REIGNITE THE PASSION

In Your Work and Your Life

Accessing contentment through

a connection to your true self

LEILA RAHEMTULLA

LEILA RAHEMTULLA CONSULTING

VANCOUVER, CANADA

This book is dedicated to those who made my roots strong and supported my growth, the ones who planted before me and to the gardens to come, and mostly to those who grace my garden right now. Thank you for your inspiration and your beauty ~ Leila.

TABLE OF CONTENTS

Introduction

Stop for just a few moments and take notice of how time passes; minute by minute and second by second, time steadily ticks by. This is your life unfolding before you. Observe it. How does it make you feel? What are your emotions and what are you saying to yourself? Are you filled with wonder and peace; do you feel your life is really amazing? Or do you feel anxiety and frustration: "Why am I sitting here *reflecting* while life is passing me by?" Or do you feel no emotion at all: "I feel nothing—I am numb. Am I supposed to feel something?" Regardless of what you feel (or do not feel), there is no denying that time is marching on. This is *your* life. Whatever you choose to do in any given moment immediately becomes your past. Life is a series of present moments; once these moments happen, they become the past—what *was,* not what *is.*

Given these thoughts, most people will still agree that they would like to live fulfilling lives. Most would love to know that their moment-to-moment activities contribute to their feeling passionate about what they do, yet when asked about their plan to do so they are a little less clear. People may want great lives, but they are not always sure how to go about creating them. And for those who know they are not on the right track, it seems hard to stop the "ride" long enough to figure out how their lives got "off the rails." Life keeps ticking by, and the chasm between wanting to live a passionate life and what is happening in any given

1

moment seems to get wider and wider. This book is about finding that connection again—reigniting your passion with your day-to-day activities so that they lead to the building of an amazing life.

The journey that is described in this book is a personal one. It is one I have travelled many times over the years. Each time I have taken on the work, it has resulted in tremendous fulfillment and joy. My hope is that each person who reads this book and commits to the work also receives these benefits. The chapters outline a process of self-discovery through reflection and activities. I encourage you to commit to this guided learning, as I have benefited greatly from it, and so have many of my students, clients and colleagues. Through discussion, dialogue and reflection, I have identified strategies for creating a "clearing" to access contentment as well as discovering ways in which "reigniting the passion" can happen in a self-study format. The purpose of this book is to make the process of reigniting passion available to a much wider audience in a self-guided format that makes it easier to put into practice.

This book is about accessing something that has always been available to you. It is about opening up possibility and living the contented life that you deserve. This process is not new. Tools of self-discovery have been available for generations, and this process has often been the root of people's explorations of their identity within their culture, their faith and their community. Although this book is written within the North American context, it draws from philosophies from around the world and the learning shared within many cultures and ages. The message about living a passionate life in each moment is not new; however, the method I describe does work in today's modern, fast-paced world—it has worked for me and for many people I have met. I think the many existing versions of this message speak to the critical need for this kind of process to be relevant. People need it to work in their "real world." The fact that many versions of this message now exist also suggests that in today's world there are many people who want to feel passionate again.

This process may not be new for you. Learning and evolution are normal parts of human development. You may have explored a version of this work in some part of your personal growth already. In doing so, some of the steps outlined in this book may be ones you have already taken or ones you recognize. That is quite common. The purpose of this book is not necessarily to teach you something new, but rather it is to set out the steps within a larger framework so that your goals can be achieved. If you are familiar with a certain step because you have done it before, know that you might be able to complete that chapter more quickly. However, as a caution, do not assume that if you have taken this step in one aspect of your life, you have taken it in all other areas. Also, be careful in your assumptions; when you think you know something, your belief can sometimes close you off from any real learning in the area. Even if a chapter looks familiar or simple, go through it, completing the activities as if they are new. Doing so may uncover something that has been missed in past iterations of the stage.

What is inside you is not new either; I believe that all people have inside them a core of happiness. It was there when you were a baby. When you were born you did not know anything but to be your self, and this "true" self has always had access to contentment. Along the way, you put on a few layers of another "self" that may be blocking the access to that core, true self. This book explains how you might clear what is getting in the way. It is important to remember that this process is not about "fixing" your life, "fixing" you, or those around you. This kind of process really means getting past the "something is wrong" mentality. In all my teaching and consulting, I have never really been comfortable with the thought of fixing people. Yet, in many cases, that is precisely why some people take a course or seek out a consultant—because they feel something needs to be fixed. My concern with the premise of "fixing" is that it implies that there is something wrong and that I am going to be the one to make it better. My hope is to contribute to a shift in your thinking, one that looks at "what is right" instead of "what is wrong" and uses what is right as the foundation of moving forward. I also want you to understand how much of this is within your own power.

Why is this shift so important? It is about approach and about managing the journey of self–discovery. Who you are before you take on this process will be more or less who you are afterwards. Some things may change for you, but ultimately this will be more about looking at who you are and very carefully tapping into what is already inside of you, rather than changing you into someone else. I believe it is unrealistic to think that reading any book can "change" you into something that you are not. All that you need is inside of you. This process will be about uncovering your true, passionate self and embracing it.

An analogy might help explain this idea. I have used analogies and metaphors throughout my career to help explain complex concepts with concrete examples; they seem to help people understand the concepts more easily. While writing this book, I have been struck by how improving your life is like growing a beautiful garden. Given this gardening perspective, the "something is wrong" mentality is like looking at a petunia and asking, "Why can't you be more like a rose? What is wrong with you?" You are who you are, and this book is about uncovering your beauty and having an understanding and connection to that beauty in a way that allows you to feel complete, joyful and content. Your access to a passionate life can only come from having a clear understanding of yourself. Using the metaphor, the goal is to discover and strengthen the "petunia" that you are, rather than to reinvent yourself as the "rose" you are not.

I have used this garden metaphor throughout the book, perhaps because much of the writing was done in my own garden. I am not a master gardener, so I am sure there are aspects of the metaphor that are not perfect. For those of you who are *real* gardeners, I apologize for any flaws in the comparison. Using the garden metaphor has allowed me to explain in much simpler terms some of the key developmental activities and stages that are required in this process. I find it easier to refer to the gardening terms when repeating some work or making reference to an activity. These analogies have helped students really *get* it. Imagine having only to say, "I am just doing a bit of *weeding* in my life"—rather than saying, "I find myself doing things that do not serve myself or others, and I think I should stop doing those things." Sometimes the metaphor is just more to the point.

This process of self-development takes courage, and I admire anyone who takes this journey on. Although this might start out as a personal journey where the goals are very much about you as an individual, the outcomes will often become the gift that you may give to all those around you. I first took this process on for myself many years ago, and I have watched as my life and the relationships with the people around me have transformed. I realize that the blessing has been having access to this process of discovery. Having witnessed how this work has created quantum shifts in the lives of others, I wanted to document it and make it available as a self-study guide. This process of self-development has been an undercurrent of many of the different courses I teach, and it is exciting to have it finally emerge and develop into a work of its own. The journey is also an iterative process—there are so many parts of your life that you can take on. With each new personal goal you can revisit this work with a fresh pair of eyes and with the confidence that the process will lay out the same steps and yet uncover an amazing new journey.

This process of self-development is about reflection and learning. A Buddhist proverb states, "When the student is ready, the teacher appears." This phrase may be about your overall journey through this book or it may pertain to the individual moments of insight or challenge. Being ready means creating an openness for the lessons and a willingness to look for the "teachable moments" in less than obvious places. Even though I have been the teacher, I have learned so much more from my students when I have allowed myself to be open to discovery and become the student; they have taught me, as have my children, my family, my friends and colleagues and even strangers. On this journey you may find your teachers in the most interesting and unexpected places; I ask you to be open about where they may be.

There may also be moments of challenge or "breakdown" through this work. I want to address this issue upfront because it may relate to your learning. My mother has a saying about difficult moments: "Even in this, there may be something to learn." Be open to what lessons may await you. Your lesson may be discovering the courage to face challenging moments in your life. Let yourself be open and you will get the most out of this book.

It is my honour to share this process with you. Dr. Wayne Dyer, in his book *10 Secrets for Success and Inner Peace,* writes, "Don't die with your music in you." That line was the inspiration for this book. This is my music. This is the music that has been inspired by the thousands of students I have had in my classes. It is the melody that has been playing in the background as I have watched leadership blossom and people develop. I am so very grateful for all those who trusted me enough to invite me to be a part of their self-development. I feel privileged to have been a part of their personal journeys. In my own work, I have been blessed with many teachers along the way; educators can be the worst students, so I am particularly grateful for those who stuck with me, believed in me, challenged me and taught me. I am so pleased that this work is in a format that takes this out of the classroom and into the world. May you be blessed on your journey. I wish you all of the best in living the life that is in you, the life that you deserve.

With gratitude,

Leila.

Chapter 1: Are you ready?
No, really, are you ready?

So here you are at the beginning. I thought the first chapter should be about making sure you are ready for this journey. Regardless of why you are here, there are a few things to get clear about before moving on. Think of this as guided study, almost a course in itself. I want to make sure you are prepared and have the things you need in place to ensure your success.

Opening this book, or even merely reading it, provides no guarantee of results—there is more to this process. If you are interested in taking this book on, the most important thing you can ask yourself is, "Am I ready? Really ready?" Being ready means that you are able to make a distinction between thinking this is a good idea and doing the work to get there. This process *will* be work. If you are merely at the stage of *thinking* a passionate life is a good idea, you would be better off spending some time daydreaming. Seriously, do not waste your time reading about this process unless you are truly prepared to take on the work.

Am I trying to scare you away? No. I just believe it is important to be upfront and honest with anyone who is interested in this process. If you commit to this development, it will be work; however, what you give is also directly related to what you get. Think of a beautiful garden; it often does not get that way by accident. Someone took that work on with intention. It may have started as a plot of wasteland or even a garbage dump or perhaps an already beautiful garden. Regardless of the starting point, any work to make it more beautiful (or to keep it beautiful) was directed effort. Using this garden analogy for your life may help you frame this process. I have no idea where you are at or what your starting point may be; your life may already be beautiful, or perhaps it is a bit unruly and unmanageable. In some ways, it does not really matter. Where you are starting from is where you are you starting from—it is what is so. Regardless of where you are, making your life better will take some work. In the early stages this process may feel overwhelming, but I promise, just as you start to see results in a garden, the effort will start to pay off. As you progress through the process, the labour will soon not feel like work at all. It will compel you forward as you start to uncover your true self and your connection to a contented life.

It may help to know how this book and this process came into being. Over the past few decades I have spent a lot of my time teaching people in the area of management, supervision and organizational behaviour. I have been witness to countless moments of inspiration—moments when learners *get it*. *Getting it* is not always about the content, per se, but rather is about the individuals having life-altering revelations about their life or work or about their insights into their true self or life purpose. In both my teaching and my consulting work, I find nothing more satisfying than to watch this process unfold. I had a moment of clarity about this while on vacation in Maui. I had promised myself, and my family that I would not take marking or paperwork with me, so I only packed my watercolours and a notepad for my "alone time." Each morning, I woke up to the sound of the surf and the birds, and I could not wait to watch the colours come alive with daybreak—those mornings in Maui were glorious. After a coffee on the lanai, I would just spend time reflecting (I had a lot of time to do so, as I belong to a family of some very late sleepers!). I started to think about why I loved my work, and I kept coming back to the moments of inspiration or the "bright sparks" that learners shared. The transformational moments I witnessed represented the "Maui mornings" of my work. What I also began to see was a pattern to the revelations, a series of steps an individual would take to get to the "aha" moment. I also realized those were the exact steps I had taken in my own development. This revealed a distinct pattern in the iterative process of self-discovery.

I started recording my thoughts about these steps, and on that trip the outline of this book and the concepts for each of the chapters were conceived. The process actually turned out to be a remarkably simple one to describe. It is one that I have lived and continue to live. The actual contents of the pages were written several years later. The fact that it was not all written shortly after that trip was one of my insights. You see, I thought I needed to be *there* (wherever *there* was) to be able to describe the journey. I thought that I needed to wait for the peaceful, quiet knowing of a contented life before I could ever profess to understand this type of development. The irony is that it has been the discord and the non-peaceful parts of this process that have taught me the most and have given me an understanding about who I am and what constitutes contentment in my life. It was then that I finally understood very clearly Ralph Waldo Emerson's quote, "Life is a journey, not a destination"; I had kept waiting to get *somewhere*, until I ultimately realized that each day, I was already *there*!

With this insight in mind, you may wish to take a moment to reflect on where this book might take you and what you think you want from it. Through this process you have an opportunity to have a good look at who you are as a person. Through the chapters and the activities you can start to uncover some truths about how you have "created your garden." You may identify patches that need a little weeding and others that need a complete overhaul. You may also find that there are some very unorthodox parts of your garden that make it interesting and different, and do not need changing at all.

Although this chapter describes some of what you might do through this process, there are a couple of important things to remember to ensure success. One is to trust the process. At times, this kind of work will feel overwhelming or may not seem to provide the results you expect. At this point, it will be important for you to keep moving through the work and not second-guess what is happening. I find this process works best with coaching, which is a lot easier face-to-face, as I can get a better sense of a person's frustration or hesitation. Since you are reading this and we are not face-to-face, I will give you this advice upfront and trust you will remember it when you feel a bit lost.

In addition, you need to make a commitment to take on the work. As I mentioned earlier, you need to make the decision to move past the daydreaming stage. This will be work, and you have to decide how you are going to approach it and how you will carve out time in your day and your life to take this work on. You will need a time of day that is yours for reading and reflection. For some, this time might be first thing in the morning; you may choose to wake up 30 minutes earlier to do a bit of work from the chapters. For others it might be the commute time, a self-imposed walk at lunch, or a commitment to watch a little less television during the evening unwind. Setting up a routine for this work allows you to get into the swing of it. You will need to give yourself time to read the chapters; however, the bigger commitment will come from your own personal reflections, journaling, or thinking through some of the activities in the chapters and, ultimately, taking the steps you outline for yourself to achieve your goals. This work will take time and diligence to provide the desired results. You will likely revisit chapters in the book because the iterative process implies that you may need to travel a certain road a few times before you are satisfied with what has come of it and where you have arrived. Choose a part of your life where the work calls to you. In gardening, the people who stick with it longer are the ones who incorporate it into their lives in a joyful way. It is not work, but rather a labour of love. Treat this as a love for yourself and the life you deserve. Create a structure that works in your life—no excuses—just complete freedom to determine how you will fit this into your day.

As you are at the beginning of this process, this is probably a good time to introduce the concept of perception. When I teach, I suggest to students that perception is "your view of the world": it is what you believe to be true. Through all of this work, it will be important to remember that your perception filters all that you evaluate and reflect upon. In my classes, I often hold up an index card that is black on one side and white on the other. I hold the black side up towards the class and ask the students what colour it is. Usually students answer black or some shade of black such as charcoal or slate. Then I look at the class and say, "You are wrong. It is white." At this point the students do not believe me, and some students question me. I carry on with the demonstration and stand my ground, even though some of the class may try to convince me otherwise. I insist that I will go to my grave believing this card is white. Usually someone will figure it out and asks to see the other side of the card, at which point I turn the card around and show the class the white side. Then I let them know this is exactly what I mean when I use the term *perception*. Our perceptions are our personal view of the world. The class and I are both correct in our versions, yet in the exercise we held polar opposite viewpoints. We were looking at the same card, yet we had extremely different opinions or versions of the card's colour. The same is true for most of what we observe in the world, including when we look at ourselves. Our view of everything we observe is our version—what we believe to be true. Someone else may see something entirely different and, in doing so, may have a viewpoint that is as drastically different as the contrast between black and white. Keep the concept of perception in mind as you do this work. I may refer to it when I want to you to have another look at some aspect of your development. I may ask you to have a look at the other side of the card or listen to someone who sees something differently than you do. In doing so, I may ask you to consider whether there is another way of looking at a situation that makes it a different story or a different version of the truth. This question may be particularly useful when you begin to consider your starting point in this process. What do you see when you look at your garden? What do you see when you look at your life?

Since these initial questions may have you start taking stock of your life, I would also like to introduce the first "support structure." When I think about supports, I like to use the analogy of a tomato cage or a stake for a seedling, which holds up the plant's new growth until the plant develops enough strength to stand on its own. During the steps outlined in these chapters, you may adopt new practices that are like seedlings or new branches of growth and you will need to support and keep them stable, healthy, and alive. The first support is to identify a way to record your progress. If you journal on a regular basis, then this first step may simply be that you invest in a new journal. If you do not journal, you may need to consider how you would like to record your thoughts. It may be that you open a file on the desktop of your computer or a note page in your handheld device. Choose a format that works for you (and release the idea that this will be the perfect system for you throughout; what starts out as a good format may not be practical or sustainable later on). Be open to adapting your recording system as you go through the process so that you can find a system that suits you. What is important, though, is that you find a place to record your thoughts and document your progress. This will be particularly important if you find that you need to repeat a chapter or a section of work. You will be able to review what you have done so far and use that as your new starting point.

Some of you may resist the idea of recording your thoughts and may say to yourself, "I am not a writer." However, this is not about writing for someone else, this is about recording your process. Capturing your thoughts in writing supports the seedling or young branch of personal development. I have found that students who take notes and complete the exercises in a written format get much more out of them. This may be the part that feels like *work* for you—it may be uncomfortable or cumbersome—but it is a critical part of staying on track in your journey. Although it may initially feel like a chore, once you find a way to record your thoughts that works for you, the activity will become easier. If you do not record you process, you are *not* doing the work. Remember the title of this chapter; if you are *really* ready to take on this work, you will establish a way to record your progress.

15

Otherwise, reading this book will just be a dreaming exercise; it may be fun, but there is no guarantee for any results.

Another structure you will need to consider is *when* you will do this work. A garden is not created with random spurts of energy, but rather with well-timed methodical steps. (Some may argue that you *can* create a garden with random, haphazard actions; however, the likelihood of success is lower and the results would be less consistent.) You will need to consider how you allocate time in your routine to move through this process. A schedule is another important support for you as a learner. In my experience, self-study students are more likely to drop a course when they have not created a reasonable and achievable schedule for themselves.

Now, if you are like me, you are probably resisting all of this structure. You may even be asking yourself, how can a creative process such as personal development come out of something that looks so ... disciplined? Understand that it is the discipline that will get the job done. Think about a beautiful creation, such as a painting or a sculpture; it takes time and discipline to complete. Without this kind of dedication the piece would remain just a dream in the eyes of the artist. Your life deserves this time, and it will be you who decides how you will do the work. Ideally, I would like to suggest that you identify the time of day when you are most inspired, alive and motivated as the time you choose to do this work. You must establish a routine that fits into your week. You may also want to identify alternate times because "life happens." As a morning person, I find getting up earlier and giving myself quiet time is particularly productive. For others, the peace at the end of the day will allow for the most reflection. Choose what is right for you, but allow yourself at least 20–30 minutes per sitting and consider working a minimum of three times per week. Just like recording your progress, this commitment may be something you resist. Again, if you are *really* ready, you will establish a realistic schedule. Making the schedule unreasonable or impossible will sabotage your progress.

Once you have got your notes area identified and a schedule that is right for you, you are ready to begin the first exercise.

THE DREAM GARDEN ACTVITY

When you are considering what you want out of your life, start with a visual of what it would look like if you could "wave a magic wand" and have the perfect life. If your life is a garden, what makes it perfect for you? What is in it? What are you doing? Who is in it? How does it make you feel?

Once you have had a chance to imagine your dream garden, I would like you to write down three goals for yourself. These goals should bring you closer to your dream or describe specific components that make the garden right for you. I have used this activity in my courses for years, and I have seen profound results. In his book *The 7 Habits of Highly Effective People*, Stephen Covey's habit #2 is, "Begin with the end in mind." That is exactly what I want you to do here. I find that when my students begin a course by identifying some personal goals it shifts their listening, and they are able to keep a personal focus on the content. The course work becomes their own and they start to identify the route to their goals. This is your chance to decide what your dream life looks like.

When you consider your goals, a good way to do it is to imagine you are at the end of the process. You have completed the book and you are thrilled with the time and effort you have put into the journey. In doing so, you have a tremendous sense of accomplishment and achievement. What is it that you achieved? What does success look like for you? Those are your goals. Do not worry if the goals are not perfect. They are not written in stone and you will have several opportunities to revisit them in later chapters. For now, just focus on getting three goals down for yourself—three things you would like to achieve as a result of the time you commit to this process. The goals could be simple, such as time for your kids, a better sense of accomplishment at work, or better time management. If these are the things that will reignite your passion and lead to a more contented life, then they are perfect. I ask you to keep it to three goals for practical purposes. I find that more than three goals can confuse the process or become overwhelming. If you have more than three, pick your top three and keep the others for another round of this process; once you understand the format and the sequence, you will be able to revisit the stages with the other goals and work through them in the same way.

Sample Goals:

1. A job that pays the bills but also feels rewarding—one that makes me want to jump of bed each day.

2. A level of physical fitness that lets me play soccer with my kids without getting winded or having my knees blow out.

3. Having time in the week to run errands for my aging parents.

The goals may be refined as you work through this process. At this stage it is important to start with your gut feeling—what is it that you want right now? Try to be specific in the outcome so you have a picture of what success would look like in each of the three goals. Personally, I find that visualization is very helpful for this. I first consider the emotions, such as contentment or happiness in a particular part of my life. Then I close my eyes and imagine what that reality might look like. As my kids were growing up, one of the visuals I had was that we would have summers truly "off"; the days would pass slowly, with no real agenda, and the summer would not be filled with appointments and obligations but rather be days at the beach or even in the backyard just playing. Having that visual was extremely useful in determining alignment in my career and life choices. The picture in my mind defined success and gave me a beacon for what I was striving for in the area of time with my kids.

Using the garden metaphor, imagine the most beautiful garden for you. For each person this image will be different, and that is precisely why this exercise needs to be done. What you do in later chapters will be driven by what you have envisioned here. You will notice that in the sample goals the descriptions are specific. I encourage you to write your goals with these kinds of descriptions rather than have more generic ones, such as "be happy at work" or "lose weight." Push yourself to really explain what that future might look like or feel like. Describe your three goals in such a way that an external observer would be able to verify, without a doubt, that you have achieved them.

As you start working on the visuals and the specifics of your goals, you may want to be cautious of your own mind's self-talk (the voice inside your head). All the reasons why your goals are unachievable or too ambitious may start to creep inside your thinking. I call these interruptions the "yeah, buts" of self-talk. Be on guard for these! This is *your* dream and *your* life—at this point, it is about "playing big." You may want to use what I call the "Greenhouse Technique" in order to isolate and protect your goals. Think about what a greenhouse can offer, a safe space where fragile or new growth has an opportunity to thrive. Seedlings in the greenhouse are protected from the elements; similarly your dreams need to be protected and need to become a focal point of attention. When you write down your goals, consider putting a box around them and list your "yeah, buts" on the outside. This creates a visual space where your goals have been separated from the self-talk.

When you had established your note-taking process and time schedule, I asked you to be reasonable. However, in this Dream Garden Activity, I ask you to consider being *unreasonable.* Do not settle here—really dream! People do not achieve their life dreams by saying, "That is impossible" or "I will never be able to do that." Look carefully into your Dream Garden, and in that visual do not be afraid to record what you see. Put those dreams into your greenhouse so they will have a chance to grow. There will be plenty of time later in the process to work out the practical details and check for what is realistic, but for now, just focus on your dream life. In the garden, for this activity, the gardener needs to focus on the beautiful outcome, not on the hours it will take, the fact that resources are scarce, or that it is possible that no one will appreciate the effort in the end. Dealing with those kinds of issues will come later on. If you start listening to the "yeah, buts" now, it may alter your goals and cause you to sell yourself short of your real dream.

THE GARDENER'S OATH

Now that you have some basic structures in place and three goals to get you closer to a dream life, I would also like to ask you to make a commitment to the process: create a contract for yourself. This is about getting clear on what you are prepared to do to achieve the results. This step can be likened to obtaining a gym membership; decide to "buy the season pass," not just show up as a "drop in." In the note of commitment to yourself address what you are prepared to put into the process: What you will give of yourself. Include how you have decided to allocate time to your process: Who do you need to enlist for support to carve out the time? This is not so that others will be accountable for your work, but rather so that you can get some help in managing your other responsibilities as you take on this process.

Consider the sample Commitment Contract listed below. Use it as an example and create wording that is appropriate for you. This step is important to take as it formalizes your intention about this work; —I promise you, you will get farther if you do this. Research has shown that when people make their goals public or "speak them to the universe," they are more likely to achieve them. Recording your commitment for yourself is a first step in realizing your goals. You may want to share this commitment with others, especially with the important people in your life. Although it is your choice to share this, if someone you trust is aware of your commitment, their awareness may provide one more support for you throughout this process.

Sample Commitment Contract:

I want to reignite the passion in my job and have decided it is no longer something I just want to dream about. I am prepared to do the work by doing the reading for 30 minutes at least three times a week on weekdays and by using my commute time to and from work to record my notes. I will be using a journal for my work and will keep it with me so I can make use of downtime for reflection. I have asked my spouse and family for support in helping me commit to the readings by having 30 minutes of quiet time for everyone with no television or video games each evening during the week. I have cleared an area in the den to create an environment that is free from distractions. I have shared my commitment to the process with a trusted colleague who has been more of a mentor to me. We have agreed to touch base on my progress on a monthly basis.

In the process, I will especially ensure I take care of myself. This work is coming out of love for myself and for all those around me. Through the toughest times, I will come back to this statement of commitment to remind myself of why I have chosen to do this work. I hope to understand my true self and to access the life that is in me—the life I deserve.

Jane Doe, November 27, 2010

You have complete freedom in what you describe in the first portion of your contract; try not to let it be too short, as the intention is to provide clarity on what needs to be in place. As well, do not create a "supreme court brief" with exhaustive plans as that level of detail may become suffocating and could end up putting you off. I suggest you write something about why you are taking on this process and a little about the "how": What framework are you building to help sustain your commitment to the work? Whose help or assistance will you need? What format is right for you to record your notes, and what schedule would be manageable in your life? Consider including in the last paragraph from the sample contract verbatim ("In this process, I will especially take care of myself … the life I deserve"). Regardless of the details in the first part of your contract, this last part should be part of everyone's commitment to this work.

One final note for your preparation: Chapter 7 is entitled, "How do you make it through a dispassionate time?" If you are working through the process and you feel it has become too difficult, you may want to jump to Chapter 7. Look at the specific sections and consider what is happening; for instance, are you skipping the work, dropping away from it, or feeling frustrated or emotional? Hopefully, Chapter 7 will give you some insight into what is happening. Once you have that clarity, return back to where you left off and continue on with the process. Again, as with gardening sometimes great plans can go horribly awry. You may need to take a moment in that breakdown to have a rethink, understand what happened, and then return to the process with that insight.

At the end of each chapter I will recap the activities from that chapter and ask you to reflect on some aspects of the content. Look upon these activities as your homework. Do not proceed to the next chapter until you have completed the activities, as they will often be the foundation of the next stage in the process.

Chapter 1 Activities

- ➤ **REFLECT**: Ask yourself if this is the right time for you to commit to this process (if not now, when? Remember, "someday" is a dreamer's answer.) What has shifted that makes this desire for fulfillment no longer a dream?

- ➤ **DO**: Ensure your note-taking structure is in place (buy a journal, set up a file on your laptop, or set up space on your handheld device). Make sure that the space you intend to work in is attractive to you in some way; setting up an enjoyable space is like investing in good tools or gardening gear before you undertake a major task in the yard. Setting up the space will also motivate you to dive into the process.

- ➤ **REFLECT**: Consider what would be a realistic schedule, something doable in your life. Ideally, it would be good to have a few minutes each day. At a minimum schedule at least three times per week to focus on the work.

- ➤ **DO**: Record your schedule of reflection time. Add your schedule to your day timer and enlist the help of those around you. For example, you may wish to tell your family that you will be shutting the door for a few minutes each day, or you may need to schedule some "me time" on weekends.

- ➤ **DO**: Record three goals for yourself as outlined in the Dream Garden Activity. Use the visualization process of imagining yourself at the end of this work. What do you see yourself having achieved? What does success look like?

Were there any "yeah, buts" in your self-talk? Check to make sure you did not understate your goals because of the self-talk. Use the Greenhouse Technique to separate out your goals from all the self-talk that might be going on for you.

> **DO**: Draft the Commitment Contract from the Gardener's Oath Activity. Outline why you are doing this work and how you will approach it. Include how you have addressed the structure of recording notes and allocation of time. You may also want to write about your openness to the journey, your trust in the process and how you will ask for support along the way. Share your contract with someone you trust if you are ready to do so.

> **DO**: Record any insights in the Bright Sparks section of your journal or personal record. Consider whether you have had these goals before. How has perception impacted your view of your life? Did perception have anything to do with your choice of goals or your ability to put the structures into place?

Having completed this first chapter, you have set the stage to bring fulfillment and passion into your life. Hopefully, these structures and the initial legwork and reflection have set you up for success. This is what you have accomplished so far: You have asked yourself if you want to take this project on and whether you can fit this into your schedule. You have assembled some of the tools and supports and defined what success will look like for you. For those of you who choose to repeat this process, remember the work may shift as you choose new goals. Your definition of success will guide your steps as you move through the process again.

Chapter 2: When you stop smiling, consider that something needs to change.

Even if you are a person with a predominantly positive outlook, you may feel that some aspects of your life could use improvement. This chapter is about taking a bit of time to explore the parts of your life that are not quite the way you would like them to be, the impact of being in an unfulfilled state and what life "not working" really means in this process. When examining the parts of your life that are not working for you it is important to watch your self-talk. After all, when you think about it, at some point *everyone* has things in their life that can cause them a little grief. I love the quote by the author Anais Nin that states, "There came a time when the risk to remain tight in the bud was more painful than the risk it took to blossom." Taking risks and feeling pain or a little grief are natural parts of living and, as you will see, they are an important part of personal growth.

In the chapter title, what I mean by "smiling" is not necessarily whether there is a silly grin plastered on your face (although for some that is what happens.) My definition refers to a relatively constant feeling of joy or happiness that occurs when you consider some aspect of your life. Sometimes, the actual smile is on the inside: it is a feeling we recognize of things *being right.* "Not smiling" then, does not always mean we are frowning. It is more about the feeling that things are *not quite right.* It might be anxiousness, frustration, anger, guilt or any number of states that seem far from contentment or happiness.

"Not smiling" can affect any aspect of your life. For example, in the context of your job, are you "not smiling" on the way to work? Think about it. Each workday, you get up and you get ready to invest a good portion of your waking hours in your job. What goes on for you when you think about a day's work? Does the prospect of getting started at your job each morning inspire you? Does it get you "pumped" and cause you to jump out of bed with an excitement that you cannot contain? If not, what *are* you feeling? If you are not sure, catch your reflection on the way to work—you will probably be able to tell. Beyond the work environment, are there some other parts of your life that have stopped you from smiling? Is your relationship with your parents, your children, your significant other or your friends stopping you from smiling? Maybe you are not satisfied with your wellness, your faith, your commitment to community or your finances. Regardless of where the smiling has stopped, this aspect of your life is an important place to start as it is going to help determine whether the goals you established in Chapter 1 are right for you. To help you understand why, let me go back to the garden metaphor.

I have been blessed with a home that has a big yard with over a hundred trees and bushes. The previous owner looked after it with great care and attention for many years. She lived on her own for much of her life and probably had more time to work in her garden than I ever will. When we bought the house almost a decade ago, we looked at the yard with *mostly* positive emotions. Although we just loved the beautiful yard, we also had a little bit of concern about how much work maintaining the garden might be. Looking back, that little concern was probably a harbinger of things to come. Since then, each spring, as the days get brighter and warmer and our gaze turns out into the backyard, we seem to go through a ritual of the same emotions. It usually begins in a positive way because there are parts of the garden that we love. Spectacular greens glow in the shadow of the big cedars, slow fireworks of spring blooms burst across the yard, and a rejuvenation is palpable, as life and movement return to the space each year. All of these truly make us smile. Invariably though, we notice something that is not quite right; something will have overgrown, fallen apart, or suffered over the winter. This bit of the garden becomes the "not smiling" part and sometimes spurs a bit of regret for getting a place with such a big yard. I need to be honest; sometimes my reaction is more than just "not smiling." Sometimes, the overgrown, falling apart parts of the garden make me just plain grumpy! However, most of the time, we work through the negative feelings and get motivated to figure things out so we will enjoy the garden in the summer and fall months. One year it might be the fence posts and another year the pond. We have released the expectation that our garden will ever be perfect, in the *Better Homes and Gardens* sense of the term. By letting go of this expectation we realized that we do not have to wait until all of the work is done to enjoy our garden; we can enjoy it while the work is in progress. "Not smiling" is an assessment and does not mean this garden is a write-off. "Not smiling" points you to the parts of your life that need your attention.

In this same way, I want you to look at the "not smiling" in your life as a signal. If you were to carefully examine a garden, you would find signals or signs that tell you whether or not the garden is thriving. When plants need water, for example, they wilt and droop, and when fruit has ripened it changes colour and hangs heavy on the vine. When you see certain signals, you may identify some work for you to do in your "garden". The "not smiling" signal is the motivator for you to get started on that aspect of your life. At this point, you are doing the assessment so that you can begin to set priorities and focus on what matters most. It is important to remember that, just like the garden, it is unrealistic to expect it all to be perfect. The signs you identify in your life may be indicators of places where you could use a little improvement. Remember they are markers to guide you, rather than expressions of a state of existence. "Not smiling" is not a description of your whole life, nor is it a forever thing. What you feel strongly about may shift over time. Part of this change may be due to your perception (is the card black or white?) and part may be due to your own evolution. As you grow and evolve your priorities, what is important to you, or how you interpret signals, may shift or change.

I also want to caution you about using the "not smiling" as an opportunity to complain about or blame the rest of the world around you. This stage is not the time to find fault in your intolerant boss, your indifferent spouse, your painful childhood or your terrible circumstances. Focusing on external factors is as useless as the conversation I sometimes have that starts with, "What was I thinking when we bought a house with a yard this size?"

Instead, this stage is a time to look—*just* look. Take stock of what is happening in all aspects of your life. Look at your life like a garden. Before you get started on any work, it is best to do an assessment. What is growing well, what needs weeding and what is definitely stopping you from smiling? This objective view will help you keep your focus and not deflect this part of your work. I will address the cause of the "not smiling" later. For now, you only want to identify the aspect of your life that you would like to work on. Start this by going through the Garden Assessment Activity that follows.

THE GARDEN ASSESSMENT ACTIVITY

Consider each of the aspects of your life listed on the following page and the continuum of Not Smiling to Smiling. To the right of each aspect of your life place an X using the scale at the top of list. You should end up with a column of Xs that will give you a visual of what makes you smile or not smile and, therefore, provides a picture of what might be important areas for you to work on at this point. There is a space below if you would like to include some other area of your life or include a more specific part of a life aspect that is already listed.

Try to be as complete as possible in the assessment. You may think you should skip some aspects of your life because you feel they do not apply or are not important; I challenge you to rate them anyways. You may be surprised by what you discover.

Now that you have rated your life, it may be worth looking at what causes you to choose a score. There is concept called Equity Theory (originally developed in the 1960s by John Adams) that I often refer to in my management work. I have adapted it a bit but like that it starts with a visual of a scale (think "scales of justice"). When life feels right or just, the scales of your thinking or psyche are in balance and you are smiling. If things start to feel out of balance, the scales start to tip, and depending on how much they tip, you begin not to smile. How much the scale tips depends a lot on you as an individual. For example, what level of unfairness or inequity might you be able to tolerate? How important is this area relative to the rest of your life? Remember this situation may be

one of *perceived* unfairness or inequity—recall the black and
white card from Chapter 1.

AREAS OF YOUR LIFE	Not Smiling	Neutral	Smiling
Job			
Health/Personal Wellness			
Family Life (Immediate)			
Family Life (Extended)			
Parenting			
Professional Development/Education			
Friendships			
Love Life			
Faith/Spirituality			
Volunteer/Community Service			
Physical Activity/Sports			
Hobbies/Expression of Creativity			

Since perception is reality, you must remember your entire assessment has been done from your perspective, through the lens of your own perception. For example, if you feel you have been overlooked for a promotion or have to work harder than your colleagues for the same pay, the scales may be tipping for you. If your boss feels promotions and workloads have been fair, there may be a difference of opinion about whether you are happy at work and a very different view of the scale and whether it is tipping. It is important to remember that this activity is only looking at your internal scales. There may still be very real injustices in this world that you face. Your challenge is to make sure your thinking does not make those obstacles bigger.

On a very personal note, our scales tipped as a family when our first son was born. Despite being excited about having a child come into our lives, when we found out he had Down Syndrome, our shock, fear and disbelief tipped the scales. As we reconciled our new reality with the life we had imagined for ourselves, we went through some bouts of not smiling. However, holding our son in our arms and looking at his beautiful face would tip us back to smiling very quickly. Through the years, when we faced new challenges, the scales would tip again. But it was always temporary. Looking at the courage and honesty our son has as he faces each day always puts any of our relative inequity into perspective. He is an inspiration, and our family has truly been blessed by his being in our lives. In fact, in this work, he is probably one of my biggest teachers.

I believe that every aspect of your life probably has an internalized version of the scales. At some point you may think something is not fair. This concept helps with a number of considerations. First of all, the assessment helps you determine where the obvious tipping is happening. This form of evaluating is what you did in the Garden Assessment: where on the continuum you placed the X signified how much the scale might be tipping. The second consideration is whether your perception is shared or yours alone. For instance, would an objective observer tip the scale in the same way or the same amount, or do you have a filter that impacts your perception and assessment? The final question is: what do the results of this assessment indicate in regards to your future action? If you discover an implied need to regain balance in the scale, will you regain that balance by looking at this moment as a fork in the road with a choice to be made? Is the imbalance a sign for you to make a shift in that part of your life? Is it a temporary imbalance that will correct itself given time? Or is it something that you accept as your new reality?

Having completed the rating and considered the concept of the tipping scales go back and review how you scored. Have you been completely honest with yourself in each area? Have you been objective? Does perception come into play? I would also like you to focus on the scores that were close to the middle. Were these scores of neutrality or numbness? Neutrality may be the physical point on the scale between smiling and not smiling, while numbness might suggest an unwillingness to assess an area of your life. Numbness might cover up a sore spot, or it might indicate something you just have not prioritized. Remember, scoring in the middle implies that the scales have already started to tip. Returning to the metaphor, in my garden, there is an area that I pretend does not exist: a side patch that more often than not I ignore. I try to avoid looking at it when we scan the yard because it has been frustrating to tackle, and I do not know where to start. Upon reflection I realize this side patch is the part of my garden that overwhelms me because it is too much to handle. I tend to focus on any other part of the garden, even areas that need no work at all. The result has been a bit of an imbalance in the work I do in the yard. If I were to look at the garden in its entirety I would see some skewed priorities, and that I have not honestly and completely assessed the garden as a whole. If I had to score this part of my garden, I might score it in the middle just to avoid dealing with it. Ask yourself if any of your ratings are instances of avoidance. Have you avoided the big stuff because it looks intimidating or seems like too much work? Have you ignored, justified, or minimized some area so you do not have to be with the level of "unsmiling" they are causing? In those aspects of your life, accept that no reaction is still a reaction and selecting a middle score may not always mean it is a neutral score. This process is about looking at your whole life. Push yourself to do the assessment carefully and completely, not so you will feel guilty about a part of your life you may have been ignoring, but rather so you will have a thorough assessment to work from in the subsequent chapters.

In addition to being aware of your perceptions and filters, try to also be aware of your self-talk. You may have quite a powerful reaction when examining yourself and your life, especially if you push yourself to look at areas you have not dealt with in the past. Self-talk can turn into something quite judgmental. Rather than just noting the signpost, self-talk can actually shift the activity into blaming, defending, or any other number of negative or deflective tracks. Examine the signposts using the Greenhouse Technique introduced in Chapter 1. Ensure that when you have isolated a part of your life that is not working, you avoid judging yourself, others, or the situation. The observation needs to be neutral: an assessment of what is so rather than of what is wrong. When you identify the aspects of your life in which you are not smiling, consider putting a box around them in your notes. On the outside, list your self-talk so that you can start to see it as separate from the signposts. Examples of my self-talk in the garden are excuses why I cannot get to the side area, blaming others for not helping, and just being too busy to take it on. Here are some samples of the signposts (signs that the scales are tipping to "not smiling") and the associated self-talk.

Sample Areas, Signposts and Self-Talk

> *Area:* My Job
>
> *Signpost:* I have become much more frustrated with customers in the last six months.

Self-Talk: It is because I have too much work to do.

No one gets how hard this job is day in/day out.

Other departments are promising the world... jerks!

> *Area:* My Finances
>
> *Signpost:* I'm behind in my bills.

Self-Talk: My spouse spends too much on the credit cards.

I don't have time to look after all of this.

My parents could afford to help out.

Area: My Wellness

Signpost: I have gained weight since I have been on a diet.

Self-Talk: The diet does not work... what a scam!

My family, friends and coworkers are sabotaging it.

I'm too stressed to stick to a diet.

What you will notice is that the signpost is an observation, while self-talk is conjecture, blaming or defending. Listening to the self-talk can justify the signpost, but where does that leave you? This process is not about justifying what is wrong with your life. It is about choosing to do something that is right for you. Separating out the self-talk will help prevent it from being a distraction as you move forward. Remember, it may have been the self-talk that contributed to the scale tipping in the first place. By separating out the self-talk you can isolate in the greenhouse what is *really* tipping the scales, and be more focused on aligning that to your goals.

In evaluating the aspects of your life that may need some work, you may also want to consider the cost of not acting: At this point, with the scales tipped, what will inaction do? Will inaction leave the scales where they are, or will they continue to tip further? This is the cost of choosing to not work on this aspect of your life at this time. You have to decide whether the scales have tipped enough to motivate you to do something differently. For some people there is safety in predictable misery, and the thought of living passionately sounds risky. It is important to remember that leading a safe and predictable life does not necessarily lead to a passionate life. It will take courage on your part to take a stand for the passion in your life. Remember the flower bud: it takes courage to bloom. Here is where the goals that you wrote will serve you well. Those goals were written by you—they are what you would really like out of your life. Now you have to explore the steps in achieving those goals, and doing so may mean that you have to actually do something differently (after all, doing what you are doing, up to now, has not helped you to achieve them!).

When considering the "not smiling" aspects of your life, think about the cost of doing nothing specifically. In work, the cost may be that you have stayed in a job much too long. In relationships, it may be that they have shifted to an unhealthy place. There may be costs for how you prioritized aspects of your life. For example, sometimes people invest in their careers at the expense of what is happening at home. By looking at your life in its entirety, consider the inaction as much as the action to see what is happening to the scales.

When you evaluate your rating, you should also consider those parts of your life that are going relatively well. Do not forget to celebrate what makes you smile and do not allow the focus on the parts that are not working to cause you to skip over or minimize the parts of your life that you love. In the garden, it can be easy to obsess on a patch that does not seem to sustain any plants, or an area that looks like a complete mess. Examining a neglected side patch should not be done at the expense of missing the parts of the garden that are quite spectacular. There are positive signals and signposts as well. Go back to the garden assessment and take a look at the areas where you are smiling. Record in your notes some of the smiling signposts as well.

After completing the assessment and re-evaluating your goals, you will have gained clarity in the area (or areas) of your life that stop you from smiling, and you will also have a better understanding of the areas in which you need to focus your attention. This chapter is about recognizing the signals and ensuring that you are reading them correctly. Separating out the self-talk is an important part of the assessment and will help keep subsequent steps on track. As I mentioned with my garden, identifying what is not working does not equate writing it off. Identifying what you would like to improve in your life should not reduce its value or your ability to enjoy it.

A final note for you when you return to this chapter: remember that this assessment is an interesting look at your life at this moment in time. This assessment will probably shift, and each time you revisit this work, the scoring might change. Consider doing the assessment in different colours and dating it each time so you can monitor how things have changed. Alternatively, you may want to record this assessment into your notes for referral should you revisit the assessment at a later time.

Chapter 2 Activities

> **DO**: Complete the Garden Assessment. In what areas are the scales tipping? Review the Garden Assessment from multiple perspectives: see both sides of the black and white card. Consider the scores in the middle: do they represent neutrality or something else? Remember that scoring in the middle still implies the scales have been tipped.

> **REFLECT**: Would an objective observer score the aspects of your life in the same way? Can you view your life through a different lens to shift your perspective?

> **DO**: Once you identify the areas of your life in which you are not smiling, record these in your notes with at least one signpost and any self-talk that is coming up for you. Use the "greenhouse technique" to isolate the signpost: draw a box around the signpost and record the self-talk on the outside of that box.

> **REFLECT**: Has self-talk or not acting on the tipping scales benefitted you? Does self-talk or inaction serve you well in the life you see for yourself? Why do you think the self-talk or inaction is happening? Are you able to separate the observation from the judgment?

> **DO**: Record the costs of you staying on the same path you are on right now. In the assessment tool, specifically look at the areas where you are not smiling and ask yourself, "If I change nothing about my life right now, what do I have to lose in this aspect of my life?" Again, it is important to be brutally honest with yourself about this: this is not a time to be in denial about what you are feeling. What do you really want? What are you lacking in life? What has you feeling

sad, frustrated or concerned? Be careful not to shift back to the negative self-talk.

➢ **DO**: Record in your notes the areas in your life in which you *are* smiling. Identify at least one signpost and spend some time being in gratitude for all that is right with your life. Here is your opportunity to acknowledge those people and things in your life that inspire you; the focus is so often on what is not working, that being grateful is sometimes glossed over—be generous and genuine in this task.

➢ **DO**: Go back to the Goals you set for yourself in Chapter 1: do you have goals in the areas that you have identified? If not, reconsider your goals or what is really causing you not to smile. Think about the aspects of your life that you might have skipped over in the assessment. This step is about choosing to invest the time to make a difference in your life. Ensure that you are prioritizing well. If you feel your goals need to be rewritten or tweaked, go through the visualization process again with the smiling assessment in mind. What would really make you smile?

➢ **DO**: Record any insights about the assessment, the scales, perception, self-talk, the cost of doing nothing and how you feel about your goals in the Bright Sparks section of your journal or personal record.

Chapter 3: When did you have passion and where did it go?

Now that you have had a look at the signposts in your life, it is time to dig a little deeper and find out where your passion went. Start by going back to a time in your life when you were *truly* passionate, joyous and contented. This is not just about recalling *moments* of joy or contentment, but rather it is about recalling when being truly passionate was your way of being. Go back to the time when you did not focus on cares or worries. For some this may mean revisiting a time in your childhood that you barely remember. What was your approach to life? How did you wake up each day? Chances are, if you go far back enough, you will identify a time when you had very little awareness of having an approach to life at all. Your purpose was just to *be*.

In this way, I believe children are much less complicated than adults. Children do not have the "baggage", which people seem to gather on the way to adulthood. As a result, children are able to live lighter and freer lives and to stay planted in the present moment. There is innocence and honesty to living in the moment, free of baggage. Children spend their days learning about the world around them—reacting, responding, interacting and *being*. When children shift their focus to the past or the future, it is not to dwell there, but rather to observe and then return to the present. Children begin each and every day with passion and maintain it throughout their day without much thought. They deal with challenges and difficulty with momentary hesitation, only to go back to their interests, focusing their attention on what gives them joy. Whether or not you can fully recall being passionate, you once lived this way too. At some point, though, you became disconnected from this way of being. This disconnection might have been a result of your ego and mind starting to develop. You may have consciously or subconsciously started to challenge this "childish" way of being. Perhaps you started to need more answers or you began to have experiences that caused you to doubt yourself or question your ideas of how the world worked. If life is a game, then your growing may have caused you to rewrite the rules. New rules meant a new game and perhaps a different approach to life for you as an adult.

Looking back, I remember recognizing this distinction between being passionate and being disconnected when our son was diagnosed with leukemia. During his treatment, we spent over a year in the oncology ward of BC Children's Hospital. In that time, I noticed a difference in how many children approached cancer compared to most adults. Each day when we woke up, we began with the worry of how we would help our son fight his battle. Each day when he woke up, it was to play… and on some days the cancer got in the way. We obsessed about "what ifs," our choices, if we had done something wrong, and about his future. Our son did seem to understand that he was sick. Most of the children in that ward understood their illness. However, the children did not seem to worry about it the same way as the adults. For many of the children on that ward, the facts of their condition were only that—facts. For these children, their cancer did not define them, and their focus was on being in the present moment. I remember looking to the children when I needed to feel joy or peace, or when I needed a reminder of what was really important.

As young people grow up, what is important for them seems to change. As people develop, I think life goes from a game played with an intimate connection in a world of innocence to a higher stakes game that seems to be played solo. Something shifts. As we age we shift the rules and start to feel more like individuals and even alone. It might be that the world that was once carefree and safe has become dangerous and scary, so we become less trusting and sometimes even cynical. This shift in rules and focus changes our approach to play. Some people are even uncomfortable with the word "play"; it is not something many adults think they *should* be doing. Some may argue that this process of growing up happens because adults are adapting to the *real world*; however, for children their world is *real* too. Perception—the black and white card—is what shifts each person's view of the world, of what works, and of what is right.

This shift in perspective has occurred in you too. As you grew up, you developed an understanding of how your world works— these are *your rules*. You built a construct about how you should lead your life, how things should be, and what is right or wrong. You said to yourself, "This is the way the game *should* be played." For example, some people believe one parent should always be at home when raising children, while others say just the opposite. Another person may have a different rule: it takes a double income to raise a family. These rules guide actions and behaviours. They may dictate the perception of what is right or wrong. When you start to rewrite the rules of the game (What *should* you be doing? What *should* you be feeling? What is the *right* job?), you stray from the ease of living that you had in your childhood. This rule-adaptation process can lead to a dispassionate and unfulfilling life. All the *shoulds* can feel a little suffocating. In the metaphor, this is like believing that there is only one correct way to garden. This belief does not take into account what you *want* to do, only what you *should* do. Who dictates what *should* be done? Is it usually not the child in you nor is it the passionate side of you. Somehow, buried underneath all of the *shoulds* are the parts of your life that are passionate and fun.

So how do you rediscover your passion? How do you reconnect with that playful, passionate self that existed earlier? The trick is to separate from the *shoulds* and rules for a brief moment. Take a closer look at yourself and ask, "What is my passion? What makes me jump out of bed raring to go?" This seems like a simple exercise; however, it is important to remain separate from the *shoulds* in life at this point. For example, avoid asking, "What *should* make me jump out of bed?" The *should* turns this exercise into one of guilt rather than clarity and discovery—essentially you get stuck in the "swamp of dispassion," and the harder you fight, the more stuck you become. This is not about fighting the *shoulds* but stepping past them in a conversation with your true self. So the question about what creates a passionate life really becomes: "If you could have anything you want, what would you grow in your garden?" You see, I do not believe your passion actually went away. I believe it still exists inside of you. It was there when you were younger, and it is inside you today. If passion does not really go away, where is it? I think it may lie dormant or perhaps under layers of baggage or *shoulds* in life. Your passion may exist as a dormant seed, awaiting the right moment to show its potential and sprout forth.

THE SEED PACKET ACTIVITY

To uncover your passion you must first take a good look at yourself. In this activity you will separate from the belief and perception about what you *should* do in your life to get in touch with the *seeds* of passion that exist inside you. You will delve under the layers of baggage and *shoulds* to rediscover your passion. The purpose of this activity is to identify what your seeds of passion look like or, more importantly, to identify what you want the final bloom to look like. Imagine being in a garden shop with hundreds of seed packets that contain the possibility of amazing plants and blooms. Which ones would you choose? Identifying the blooms in their full glory guides your choice.

Imagine your *real* passion in its full glory. Consider what draws you to focus on the areas of your life that you have chosen to work on. Identify at least one aspect of the experience or the outcome that is a driver of your joy and contentment. Describe the seed packet as the most beautiful thing that you can imagine in that area of your life. Make your description clear and compelling so that you want to pick up the seed packet immediately and say, "That is what I *really* want in my garden."

This activity may take a bit of time, especially if you have been disconnected from your passion for a while. This activity requires that you really tap into what brings you joy and then imagine what the future may hold if you planted that seed.

Be aware of your self-talk. If you begin this activity and all you see is a garden that needs hours of hard work, and you believe the garden will still never be great, then you are stuck. The guilt of what you have not done and your current state is keeping you from delving down deep and discovering your passion. Let the guilt go, for just a moment, and you will uncover what drives you and what you were once connected to years ago. Use the Greenhouse Technique to isolate your seed packet from the self-talk.

Examples of Seed Packets

> Area: Love Life
>
> Growing old together with my best friend.

Self-Talk: I'll never find that person. So far everyone I have dated is a jerk!

> Area: Faith
>
> The knowing that comes with enlightenment.

Self-Talk: I can't even sit in prayer for 10 minutes, how will I ever get to "knowing"!

> Area: My Home
>
> My home is a place filled with love and is welcoming!

Self-Talk: This place is a dump, no ever helps me clean up!

In this activity, separating out the self-talk is particularly important. The samples only provide one statement for the self-talk, but you may have several statements in each area. When you create the cover of your seed packet isolate what you see as ultimately possible in the area of your life. It is important to recognize that whatever you plant in your garden will be what grows, even weeds. Keep the seed packet description as positive and clear as possible. The self-talk can infiltrate this activity, as it probably has in the past without you knowing it; doubt, guilt, or negativity may have taken over this area of your life. Having a part of your garden that you had so much hope for look neglected or overgrown can become disheartening. Completing the Seed Packet Activity is about starting over again; you begin by deciding what you want to plant and by being mindful of the self-talk that tries to self-seed along side the seeds that contain your dreams or ideals. Continuous self-talk ultimately turns into the beliefs and perceptions that shift your view. The rules or *shoulds* start to get rewritten and impact what grows in your garden.

Planting self-talk in your garden is a good example of Robert Merton's concept of the "Self-Fulfilling Prophecy." If you believe and say every day that your job is terrible (or even mediocre), these statements and beliefs will adjust your perception and how people view you in your job: you will manifest the reality that your job is terrible. Part of this activity involves looking at what you are putting out there in the universe: What are you saying to others? In his book *The Power of Intention*, Wayne Dyer suggests, "When you change the way you look at things, the things you look at change." This is quite a simple phrase, but it can help identify what happened to cause the shift. You might have started out thinking your job was good or okay, but as your perception changed the shift also affected everyone around you. In my classes, I caution managers and supervisors about the power of their beliefs and statements: if managers believe their employees are "losers," their belief will shift the relationship they have with their employees, and even the best employees will start to pull back when they pick up on this belief. Why bother trying if your boss already has a negative opinion of you? On the flip side, believing that your employees are "stars" has the same effect. A neutral or even disengaged employee may approach his or her job differently if their boss holds such a positive belief. This is not to say that our beliefs or statements can work instant miracles, but we certainly cannot underestimate the power of words in creating the world and the path that we are on. Remember the power of perception and its implications: Holding a positive belief or speaking positively may just be a matter of turning the black and white card around to look at the other side.

THE SOIL ASSESSMENT ACTIVITY

Identifying the impact of self-talk and how perceptions are influenced by the self-fulfilling prophecy involves looking at the soil as much as the seeds. In the Seed Packet Activity you described passion in full bloom. It helped you pick the seeds. Now you will take some time to see where the seeds are landing. This requires you to look at the *rules* (or *shoulds*) that have been created in your life. These are the layers that are sitting on top of the seeds or at least the medium in which the seeds are being sown. In a garden, soil is an important growing medium, as it provides the protection and nourishment for a seed to sprout. However, if the seeds are buried under too many layers or if the soil is non-porous or toxic the seeds may not sprout or thrive.

So what are the layers in your life? What kind of soil is in your garden? The soil represents your beliefs, your perceptions, and your rules of conduct for your life. When you were young and unaware of your perception or the rules, you did not need to think much through. Once you became more analytical and aware of the world and how people and things interact you made some decisions about how things work; you decided what is fair, what should be, and what makes you happy or not. You also wrote a set of rules about what you *should* do and what is *right* or *proper*. For instance, through my upbringing, I was taught that a clean and tidy home was a reflection of who lived there: messy meant uncaring, sloppy, and undisciplined among other things. I adopted this rule. My beliefs about having a tidy home were a thick layer of judgment on top of the seeds of building a loving home. Over the years, this layer of judgment was often a source of panic for me (and every now and then this self-talk still rears its head). I felt that if my house was not perfect, then whoever visited may think that I am uncaring, sloppy and undisciplined. The tidy-house rule was a crazy rule, and yet it was a real layer. Rationally, I knew that anyone visiting me already had an opinion of who I am, and the state of my house was not really going to influence that, but I would still react and feel panicky! It was not a very productive layer, as it did not fuel any passion for cleaning the house. It just felt like a lot of pressure. I would still worry about dust bunnies and what their existence said about me as a person. "Building a loving home" was having trouble thriving in all of that. Examining the rules and judgments allowed me to separate the frustration or lack of contentment about the house and ask myself, "What is really bothering me here and what do I want to do about it?" For me, I needed to truly separate out the judgment of others and ask myself, "What makes me happy in my home?" What I wanted to bloom in my home was, "A place filled with peace and love": this was my version of the description on the cover of the seed packet.

The soil assessment for the "home" part of my garden involved reflecting on the judgment and guilt that impacted whether the seeds would thrive. Doing a soil assessment showed me that I loved a clean house and needed to recognize that I did not always have time in my schedule to keep my home tidy and organized. Hiring someone to help clean the house was one of the ways we addressed this issue; this helped to create a place where my "home" seed could sprout and the possibility of the dream for our home could bloom. In doing the Soil Assessment Activity it is important that you focus on specific aspects of your life; this is akin to picking a place in the garden that needs work. Sprouts starting to grow in the patch that you have focused on will create little *wins* or "pockets of excellence." These *wins* are helpful, as they allow you to see that your passion was a dormant seed that needed a special environment in which it could grow.

If your job or career is one of the areas of your life that you intend to work on, consider whether you evaluate people by what they do or where they do it; for example, if a person works in a corporate office or is in a particular industry, it is of value? If a person makes a particular level of salary or has special perks, does that make them a better person? Do you apply these rules to yourself? Assessing these rules or perceptions can often be helpful in uncovering some less fertile layers in the soil. The rules and judgments can suffocate you or keep you trapped because they can cause you to feel dissatisfied with your life as it is. The rules may be stopping you from choosing a different path. For instance, I personally believe all jobs are valuable; however, if you have judgments about what is important or valued or what constitutes a good job, you may be limiting your choices. Do you have judgments about so-called menial jobs or tasks? I challenge you to eliminate these jobs from your organization and see how well your company runs. Think about maintenance staff and how your office would look like if no one cleaned the washrooms for a few days. Think about the mailroom and how you would operate with no packages, deliveries, or urgent couriers in your office. The cleaning and mailroom jobs may not be for everyone, but I believe that there are individuals that value doing that work and appreciate when others value their contribution to the organization. These examples may help you examine what beliefs or constructs exist for you when you think about reigniting the passion in your work.

Using the seed packet covers you developed earlier, consider where these seeds are being planted. Do a soil assessment and look for toxicity. Are there any rules, judgments, or beliefs that may be affecting whether the seeds will thrive? Look carefully at the layers, as sometimes they have been your opinions or judgments for so long they appear to be facts. The assessment for toxicity focuses on what might be hindering the seeds from sprouting or the plants from blooming. When you think about the beautiful image on your seed packet, what belief or judgment gets in the way?

As you examine the soil where the seeds of your passion are planted, think about your self-talk. Has your self-talk led to some larger set of beliefs or rules in the area of life you are considering? Compare your self-talk to the soil assessment. Has the quality of the soil been affected by the self-talk? Is this the source of the toxicity? Has the toxic soil gone back and influenced the self-talk? Is the environment where the seeds have been planted choking out the sprouts? Have other people influenced your beliefs about what you can achieve or what is possible? Are there stories you tell yourself about what you can achieve?

Examples of Soil Assessments

Area: Love Life

Growing old together with my best friend.

Toxic Soil: True love exists only in fairy tales.

Self-Talk: I'll never find that person. So far everyone I have dated is a jerk!

Area: Faith

The knowing that comes with enlightenment.

Toxic Soil: No one has proven that God even exists!

Self-Talk: I can't even sit in prayer for 10 minutes, how will I ever get to "knowing"!

Area: My Home

My home is a place filled with love and is welcoming.

Toxic Soil: Building a home is the mom's job.

Self-Talk: This place is a dump, no ever helps me clean up!

This analysis is an important step, and will continue in the next chapter. For now, be sure that you have clearly described the seed packets and had a preliminary look at the soil. At this point you may feel a bit lost. Take your time with this step, complete the activities and come back to them a few days later. If you still feel stuck refer to Chapter 7, as the sections in that chapter may help. You may need to go back and review your dream garden and determine whether your assessment was your own or based on others' opinions or beliefs. Trust yourself, you know what makes you passionate, and consider letting all the thinking go. Pick the seed packets that really call to you, and be aware of where you are planting those seeds.

Chapter 3 Activities

➢ **REFLECT**: When did the passion exist for you? Can you remember it? Can you recall when things shifted for you? There may be several incidents or times in your life where you recall living passionately.

➢ **DO**: The Seed Packet Activity. Choose each area of your life and be specific about what that area of your life looks like when you achieve your goals. You started this activity in your Dream Garden Activity in Chapter 1, but now you are describing each of the blooms in detail. Describe these blooms in a way that makes you smile and so that you feel inspired. Remember to isolate the self-talk about this area outside of the seed packet using the Greenhouse Technique.

➢ **REFLECT**: Where did the self-talk come from? Can you put the self-talk aside and focus on your goal?

➢ **DO**: The Soil Assessment Activity. Has your self-talk become rules that you live by? Does your self-talk, judgments, and beliefs impact where the seeds land? Record the beliefs that exist for you. Analyze where these may have come from and challenge them with an objective and rational mind. You may want to do the Soil Assessment Activity several times because there are usually a few layers there!

➢ **DO**: Record any insights about your passion and your rules in Bright Sparks section of your journal or personal record.

Chapter 4: Who defines perfect?

In the previous chapter you started to assess the soil in your dream garden. To do this you evaluated the layers that may be impacting the growth of the seeds. One important part of the soil analysis involves looking at your definition of perfection. How do you define it? Each person has his or her own version of perfection, and it is the bar that is used to measure satisfaction or achievement level. A good question to start with is, "Whose level of perfect do you live by?" Is it yours, your parents', your colleagues', your friends', or society's? The version of perfection is an interesting indicator and may provide some insights into the rules that you identified in Chapter 3. You may begin to uncover the source of the influences in your life, be it your own thinking or the thinking of the people who have impacted you.

The garden example will serve well here. When you decide to grow a garden, at some point you are faced with the question, "How will I know it is beautiful?" Do you hold your garden up to the standard that you have set for yourself, to a standard that has been set by others you know who have gardens, or do you look at magazines and compare? This comparison activity can leave you less than satisfied; after all, it is quite easy to find a friend, neighbour, or a magazine spread that has a garden more breathtaking than yours. Do other gardens make yours less perfect? The same thing happens in your job, in your family, and in your life choices. You can get caught up in the thinking, "Is this good enough?" The great part of that question is that it creates a very powerful drive for achievement within you. Competition can be a powerful motivator. However this drive can also go from being your servant to your master. Competition can be a double-edged sword that leaves you feeling like you will never measure up.

Understanding this dilemma of perfection (being both motivating and crushing) is an important part of this step in the overall process. Examining your ideas of perfection allows you to see the challenge you face by setting a bar that is unrealistic or perhaps not even relevant. Examining these ideas also forces you to look at why you created this definition of perfect for yourself; this may shed some light on your fundamental insecurities and the areas where you feel most vulnerable. This chapter is not about denouncing the drive that has built the life you now live. It is about recognizing that the drive has its pros and cons. Striving for perfection can energize you to better yourself and to learn, but it can also leave you feeling dejected or that you have missed out somehow.

North American culture has probably contributed to the bar you use to measure perfection. Most people in today's society compare themselves to others. "Keeping up with the Jones'" is alive and well and continues to fuel an evolving definition of perfection. Advertising, the media, and pop culture all contribute to the mindset of striving for something more. Poor people wish they were rich, and the rich wish they were richer. If a family owns one car, they want two; if they have two bedrooms in their home, they want three. People are bombarded with information about the lives of others (either real or fictional) that leaves them looking at their own lives with a level of disappointment. These types of comparisons create a "swamp of dispassion." Most likely, at some point in your life, you have thought that things, money, or even circumstances will result in satisfaction. I will not go into tirade about consumerism, conspicuous consumption, and materialism; however, I feel it is important that each person look at their own beliefs about consumption as contributing factors to their thinking.

Does putting aside comparisons mean that you denounce striving for anything? Not really—you need to earn a living, feed yourself and your family, and you need a roof over your head. You have a right to want these things in your life. Perhaps what needs to be challenged is the source of the drive. Looking behind the reasons and exploring what drives you may help shed some light on the challenge here. Are you driven to do something because there is a genuine desire to improve your life or wellbeing or are you driven because of a false belief or hope that this change will provide satisfaction levels that currently do not exist? The latter may be moving you to a twisted version of perfection and creating soil in your garden that does not necessarily encourage seeds to flourish.

A distorted version of perfection (based on comparing yourself to others or based on amassing material objects) makes it difficult for you to truly be passionate and feel fulfilled. Imagine looking at a family loving their vacation—you might say to yourself, if I spend that money on a similar trip then my family will be that happy too. When you look at it carefully, it is an unrealistic connection between the vacation and the happiness, which only serves to put pressure on all of you. It would be like saying, "If I throw X dollars for X experience, then everyone in my family should be that happy"—this is not realistic. Happiness, passion, and contentment do not have a specific price tag, and in some cases they do not have a price at all.

The relationship between perfection, comparison, and drive is not a simple one. Many people struggle and try to pull themselves out of the sticky swamp of comparison and interpretation towards what will make them happy, and then find that the comparison has pulled them back into the swamp again. I have done it myself. I have a weakness for shoes and clothes. I get a little self-indulgent euphoria when I find a great pair of shoes or an outfit— I am tempted by the belief these will make me happy. I have accepted that my reaction is not long-lived and despite usually loving the purchases, I know that I cannot look to them for joy or happiness. For other people it is cars. What is a car to you? Is it a mode of transportation for you or your family? Or is it a status symbol, a badge of honour or a statement about your commitment to the environment? At the end of the day, will your car choice contribute to your satisfaction (or dissatisfaction) with your life? I often remind my students who are parents that kids do not go into therapy later on in life because their parents did not have the nicest car. Acquiring certain things as a route to happiness may be a rule you wrote for yourself. Despite evidence to the contrary, you may continue to reinforce that rule with self-talk. Furthermore, you may start influencing others, and you may impact how your friends, children, and colleagues write *their* rules. It is important to recognize that your rules and your definition of perfection impact the soil in your garden.

The power your rules have over you was introduced in Chapter 3 with the Self-Fulfilling Prophecy. You have spent your life learning about the world and trying to make sense of it all. You establish the rules as what you believe to be true. The construct is based on your own perception. In the case of contentment or satisfaction, if you decide that you will never be happy until you have a particular car or job or until you earn a certain number of dollars per year, then that will be the framework that you operate within. However, if you take a moment to jump out of that set of rules, you can easily identify people who do not have any of those things and are living a fully passionate lives. Similarly, you can find people who have all of those things and yet still seem troubled, anxious, or wanting more.

You cannot "hang your hat" on the *things or circumstances* as the access to your happiness. Yet in North America, this has been the basis of most promotion and advertising. Organizations no longer sell a product or a service; they sell you a dream. If you buy this vacation, your family will be closer; if you are in this income bracket, you will live an elite life. Somehow these promises are supposed to make you feel good and it may be true for a fleeting moment in the relative scope of your life, but there is no guarantee for lasting happiness. Yes, there are moments when your family bonds on a vacation, which can provide a lifetime of wonderful memories; however, there are also family vacations that are so stressful and tense that the only lasting memory is the misery of being stuck in a strange place with no way out until the vacation is over. I think it is better to work on the bond or the connection with a passionate life outside of a materialistic viewpoint. You cannot throw money at a family relationship and expect that you will have long-term satisfaction. Building a strong family bond takes work. It is not instantaneous. If you can redirect your effort, and not waste resources looking for instant results, you are probably going to get better results in the long run. Creating a beautiful garden also takes time, effort and commitment. Sure, you can easily transform a space by going to a garden centre and bringing home carloads of flowering plants and accessories; however, if you have not tilled the soil and do not water the plants, the gorgeous garden will not last long. The plants will die and the weeds will overgrow all the beautiful stepping stones and gazing balls you may have carefully placed in the space. Looking for quick fixes in reigniting your passion may just serve to add to the mess that gets created before you.

If you want to build a strong family bond, you cannot achieve it in one or two weeks out of the year. Genuine bonding means investing time in the relationship on an ongoing basis; it means getting past some of the "rules" that you have written and getting clear about your intentions. This is not just a matter of saying, "I *want* this goal." It is about getting clear on what actions may be either contributing to or hampering your achievement of your goals. Your wasted energy is an important consideration. What is it that you invest in for happiness? Have you ever found yourself trying to buy a dream in hopes that it will make you feel better? Did it work? There may have been a brief moment of happiness; however, I do not believe that buying a dream will get you in touch with what *really* makes you happy. Think about the things you have accumulated or circumstances you have tried to create in different areas of your life. If you find that you have bought things you have never used or did not have long-lasting value in those experiences, consider that there might be some wasted energy or misdirected focus in reaching satisfaction or contentment.

THE GARDEN COMPARISON ACTIVITY

This activity helps you to see what influences or drives your life choices. There are times when comparing yourself to others can stop you from accessing what truly makes you passionate. You will need to separate what *you* want from what others make you *think* you want. This activity involves looking at your core reason for picking a certain dream or for defining success (or perfection) in a certain way. In this activity you pare away some of the energy you waste building the garden that is driven by the wrong reasons.

To get in touch with your true self, start by looking at what drives your real desires. At this point you have worked on your dream garden and the full glory blooms of your seed packets. Now you need to take another look at it all. How much of this dream is fueled by comparing yourself to others and how much is what you really want for yourself? How much of this has a price tag and how much of it is priceless?

For each of your goals, identify any external comparisons you were making when you established it.

Sample

Goal: I want to make a 6-figure salary
External comparison: My parents and my siblings all made 6-figure salaries, and I will look like a loser if don't achieve this.

Goal: I want to find the love of my life.
External comparison: My friends are all married or with someone. I am the only single one left.

Goal: I want to lose 20 pounds.
External comparison: Our society is focused on skinny. I am tired of being called chubby.

Doing this comparison hopefully sheds some light on the factors that have influenced your initial goal. Ask yourself, "Is this goal what I really want? Am I trying to keep up with the Joneses?" Am I trying to please someone else? Do I choose this because I feel guilty or pressured? This activity may cause you to go back and rethink your seed packets. I encourage you to consider the next activity before you return to Chapter 3 to rewrite the goals and descriptions on your seed packets.

THE MICROSCOPIC LOOK AT YOUR GARDEN ACTIVITY

The previous activity allowed you to identify some of your external influences. Now spend some time considering what you really value in your own garden. It is important that you examine the value from only your own perspective. What is it that you really value? What are the things that make you smile? Look for the things that cost nothing. At the core of each area of your life that you have chosen to study, identify something that you value because of itself and not as it is when comparing it to anything else. What do you love for no reason other than it feels right? For each area of your life start with the phrase, "I love…"

Sample

Area: My wellness
I love the invigorated feeling I get from working outdoors.

Area: Professional development/education
I love the prospect of learning something new and challenging!

Area: Love life
I love being with someone who laughs with me.

The "I love" statements from the microscopic look at your garden are glimpses of your real passion. This activity may take a while, and uncovering the core of your passion may take a few iterations. It is also possible that you do not need to rewrite your goals at all. This activity is not about finding something to change; rather it is about taking a microscopic look to uncover your real passion. Keep in mind that an important part of the work is to define perfection for yourself. Joy did not come with a price tag when you were young, and I challenge you to find the core of your joy in something that is free. When you look at your goals, did you define success (or perfection) by what was truly *your* passion or by what you think you wanted based on someone else's definition of success? What is on your seed packet? Your seed packets need to really describe what you love and not what you *think* will make you happy. They should not be about what you can purchase or obtain to be happy. While the goals may remain the same, most people need to make minor adjustments that create goals and definitions of full bloom that are more relevant, meaningful, and connected with their true selves. See if there is a way to rewrite your goals with this refined version of perfection. Do the same for each of your seed packets (see Chapter 3).

Does paring away the energy wasted on comparisons and redefining perfection provide a guarantee that your life will be perfect? Absolutely not! However, who you are and how this process impacts you will shift. You will need to be careful not to confuse living passionately with living perfectly. They are not the same. Your journey to passionate will not always be a smooth ride.

Recall I started this book while on vacation in Maui. Despite a few hiccups in actually going on this vacation, we assumed once we got to the island it would all be picture-perfect moments of family bliss! Yes, there were many of those … after all it *was* Maui. However, we also had some less than stellar family moments of disagreements, frustration, and discord. Did this mean our family was broken? Did it mean that we failed in finding our passion? Well, in those moments, it certainly crossed my mind, yet if I looked at all the obstacles we had overcome to make it on the trip I knew we were anything from broken. I was on a beautiful island with the three people that mattered the most in my life. What I realized in Maui was that real families have real disagreements and moments of discord. There is perfection in this imperfection. Getting connected with your passion is what makes it perfect.

THE CLEANING UP A MESS ACTIVITY

Reigniting passion can sometimes involve disagreements and discord, so what do you do about them? How you deal with less than perfect moments on the journey to reigniting your passion? You will need to be accountable for what gets created around you when you are striving to live a passionate life. There are times when your words or actions may impact others in a negative way and you have a bit of a mess in front of you.

I use the phrase "cleaning up a mess" a lot in my teaching. This phrase refers to the fact that people can often start communications with good intentions, but end up saying or doing the wrong thing. It can be an emotional response or a reaction that results in hurt feelings or drama. Sometimes it is self-talk that oozes out, or it may be the pressure felt when being forced to adopt someone else's idea of perfection. In all of these situations words and actions can have the potential to hurt others. If you create a mess, you need to have the grace to make amends. This is not about keeping an "I'm sorry" in your back pocket to justify future words or actions; rather it is about taking responsibility for your words and actions when they have caused hurt. Even with the best of intentions, a mess can happen. Cleaning up a mess means getting past analyzing who was right or wrong and taking responsibility for the hurt that you have caused. Cleaning up a mess sometimes means affirming the importance and value of a relationship and recommitting to that as being more important than that one conversation or incident. It is very important to be careful in the cleaning up of a mess; do not do this as a self-righteous activity or in a condescending way that implies "I am more mature and evolved than you and therefore I will be cleaning up the mess." That attitude will defeat the purpose and just be a sneaky way of trying to justify the mess rather than to take responsibility for it.

You may find that once you have made amends and cleaned up a mess that you have found resolution and feel complete but the other person is not ready to accept your apology. Cleaning up the mess does not mean that you must make the other person feel okay. It means taking responsibility for clearing up the issue and then being gracious enough to give the other person the time and space to resolve the issue on their side as well.

Are there any messes to clean up in the areas of your life that you have focused on? Have you put pressure on your friends or family? Have you said or done things that come from your own frustration and ideas about perfection? If so, remind yourself that accessing the joy in your life may come from cleaning up those messes. A mess is like leaving a big pile of garbage in front of a beautiful flowerbed. Even though your intention was to create the lovely garden, in getting there you left a distracting eyesore for all to see. Enjoying the flowers will be easier and more satisfying if you take the time to clean up the mess in front of them.

When examining your dream garden and your seed packets stay focused on what is important to you and accept that not everything will be perfect. The garden does not need to be perfect, and if you wait for perfection you may miss the beauty of the garden as it is right now. When I did the garden comparison and the microscopic look at my garden activities in my own yard I realized how much the earlier views of my garden had been tainted by picture-perfect yards. I would zero in on what was wrong and how that area of my garden did not measure up. When I shifted my perspective and looked at the garden in isolation—without any comparison—it became an amazing, beckoning backyard. In the microscopic activity, my "I love" statement was: "I love the hundreds of shades of green and the range of textures and the fact that a space could create peace." In fact, while writing this book I found out that the word "paradise" comes from the Old Persian term for "walled garden." How appropriate! When I looked past the weeds and the parts that needed work and focused on the textures and colours that I loved, my garden was truly paradise.

The work that you have done in this chapter not only helps you create a better quality of soil, it also helps you determine exactly what seeds to plant. By redefining perfection on your seed packets, you are refining what you plant in your garden and are getting closer to achieving your goals. Making sure the soil is good creates a much higher likelihood of success.

In the areas of your life, you want to look for the paradise and touch on the part of your life that really calls to you or that makes you feel connected in an inspirational way. You are getting closer to your own definition of perfect and, in doing so, shedding much of the self-talk. Work on looking past the self-talk and focus on noticing the parts of your life that give you joy. You may not be able to completely quiet the self-talk, and there may be times when it still comes up and impacts what you say or do. When this happens, remind yourself of the perfection of imperfection. Refocus, clean up any messes, and commit to achieving the goals that really matter to you in your life. This process might not be easy for you, and it may take a few iterations for you to really live a passionate life. This work entails being open to self-evaluation, being vulnerable enough with those who know you, and being brave enough and humble enough to apologize when you make a mess. This can be a complex process; however, the payoff is huge.

I have seen this part of the process create quite a transformation. It is truly inspiring for me to see students begin to pare away the comparisons and the self-talk and uncover their own paradise and begin to live a passionate life.

Chapter 4 Activities

> **REFLECT**: Who defines "perfect" for you, and what is your definition of "a good life"?

> **DO**: Complete the Garden Comparison Activity and the Microscopic Look at Your Own Garden. Record your goals and what outside comparisons may have influenced why you chose that goal. Are these really your goals, or are they someone else's? When you microscopically look at your garden try to identify in each area that you are working on as a description that has no price tag or no comparison.

> **REFLECT**: How much of what you have already achieved or acquired in your life has come because of how you wrote the rules or your definition of perfection? Can you differentiate between the driver of your desire and the driver of "keeping up with the Joneses"? Can you accept

your own version of perfection? Can you accept the perfection of imperfection?

> **DO**: Rewrite or adjust your goals and your seed packets in a format that has no price tag and does not make a comparison. Record any insights in your Bright Sparks section of your journal or personal record.

> **REFLECT**: Consider whether or not you have created a mess anywhere in the areas of your life that you have chosen to work on. Have you said or done something that you know was wrong or that you regret?

> **DO**: Engage in the Clean Up A Mess Activity. Record the mess and how you approached cleaning it up. What was the outcome? Did the person's response to your cleaning up the mess surprise you? Did that person's acceptance or non-acceptance of your actions to clean up the mess impact whether you felt a sense of resolution? What did you learn about yourself in this activity? Has this kind of experience impacted the quality of your soil or the rules that you have for yourself?

Chapter 5: How does your garden grow?

Much of the work done up to now was to ensure you were headed in the right direction. Now you will actually start the work involved in reaching your goals: This is the point where you roll up your sleeves, jump into your garden, and get to it! As you plant the seeds of your goals, you will also need to plan for the growing process. You will have to consider how you will keep the seedlings alive. You may have to establish new routines and activities. These actions may represent new territory for you. You will need to recognize that focus or attention may not be enough to keep you moving and energized towards your goal. You may also need to establish new structures in your life to ensure you stay on track. In doing so, you safeguard and strengthen the process of achieving your goals.

THE ESTABLISHING SUPPORTS ACTVITY

You planted the seeds in good quality soil; now you must determine how to incorporate the care of these seedlings within the rest of your busy life. Remember there are parts of your day that you cannot let slip (and perhaps some that you can). Look at how you can support the achievement of your goal within a day that is probably already full. Look at the structures (i.e., activities and routines) that can support your goals and what you need to pare back: in the garden, you are staking your tomatoes and pruning back the vines. Take into account the daily and weekly activities, such as watering and feeding, that are necessary parts of your commitment. As you work towards your goals, consider what needs to be in place.

In this activity, consider the goals you have set for yourself. Work backwards and determine what is needed to reach those goals. What structures do you need to establish so you can achieve them? By answering this question in each area you have chosen you will start to identify what steps or specific commitments you need to complete to move you closer to your goal. Complete the following sentences for each of your goal areas.

To achieve my goal I need to make time for...

A structure that would work for me to achieve this is...

My biggest challenge to sticking with this will be....

Therefore, to safeguard the structure I am....

Specific commitments I can now make are...

Sample:

Aspect of my life: Promotion

To achieve my goal I need to make time for my own personal development. I will have to determine the skill set I need for the advancement and also identify where possibilities for promotions exist either in my own organization or elsewhere. I need to work on my own self-confidence; if I don't believe I deserve this, no one else will.

A structure that would work for me to achieve this is to research what is required for me to be promoted from my current position. I need to speak to my boss or someone in HR as well as find a mentor who has travelled a similar career path. I need to look at taking courses to develop my skills as well as demonstrate my initiative and desire for advancement. I need to also look for opportunities to develop my skill set on the job if possible and work on getting feedback from others about my capabilities.

My biggest challenge to sticking with this will be making the time for this given everything else that is going on in my life. As well there are limited possibilities in my organization and it's not really an environment that promotes employee professional development. I'm not sure how my boss will react. Will he think I want his job? In addition, there are not a lot of mentors that I can identify at work. I have to watch my self-talk; I tend to be hard on myself in any kind of performance evaluation.

Therefore, to safeguard the structure I am going to widen my possibilities to organizations within my industry (and even beyond). I will still talk to HR and my manager on what courses or kinds of opportunities may be most suitable, but I'm going to start looking outside my organization. In order to make time for this, I am going to ask for help from my family because courses or even volunteer work may have to be in the evenings, and knowing that some of my obligations at home are temporarily addressed will help me feel good about committing to the development. As for finding a mentor, I commit to attending industry events where I can speak to more individuals and learn about other organizations. I will also work on quieting the negative self-talk and catching myself when I go there.

Specific commitments I can now make are:

1. Within the year I need to do one thing under the area of personal or professional development. It needs to be specific enough to add to my resume (e.g., taking a specific

course, accepting a volunteer position, or attending a conference).

2. Attend at least two industry events (conference, lunch, or other networking opportunities) this quarter to network.

3. Identify two possible mentors within six months, discuss my willingness to learn and desire to be promoted with them, and ask for their advice on how I might proceed.

4. Redo the Greenhouse Technique to focus on the self-talk that tends to convince me not to proceed.

5. Earmark funds for the course/development opportunity should it not be approved by work. (I will arrange for a $20/week transfer from my chequing account to a professional development fund.)

6. Include my family and ask for their help in achieving this goal. Get their help on the nights I'm away and allow me to take time to study or work on weekends.

This activity is about testing your own intentions in wanting the goals you identified. You may have tweaked your goals or what success looks like several times since the start of the book. There is nothing wrong with that. Refining your outcome likely means that you are paying more attention to the journey, and you are clearer about where you would ultimately like to end up. It is quite possible that by starting on the specific commitments, you have an insight that causes you to change your course dramatically. As long as the new seed packet is what you really want and not sabotaging self-talk or procrastination, then that is fine. Try to be as honest with yourself as possible. The seed packet is yours to define (and redefine).

This work is also about eliminating the excuses for why you have not yet achieved these goals. Chances are it was fairly easy to list the specific commitments required. Now ask yourself, why you have not done these things sooner? Perhaps the goal was not enough of a priority in your life, or perhaps other things came up. If this goal is something that you *really* want, then acknowledge that you allowed the goal to somehow shift from goal back to daydream. Now it is time to bring the goal back again—a real goal with real actions. This work is about looking within and removing some of the blocks that did exist as well as creating the supports so that reaching your goals becomes both intentional and possible.

Supports may also change as you move towards achieving your goal. Consider what is required to hold up a young tomato plant: It only needs a small stake to support the main stem. As the plant matures, however, a tomato cage is required to hold up the branches that will soon be heavy with fruit. The earlier support— a small stake—is not enough. As you evolve towards your goal, your original supports may no longer serve you. Consider setting timeframes to periodically reevaluate the structures; ask yourself whether the support is still working or whether another support needs to be in place for you to continue working towards this goal.

With the promotion example above, the original support may have been an investment in education by taking one night school course. Down the road, it may be that—in order to achieve the goal imagined—a degree is required. Carving out the time, resources, and commitment to earn a degree requires a much larger set of supports than just attending one class. The financial piece alone may require a more complex strategy. In addition, family members may be reluctant to shoulder commitments in this longer time frame and other arrangements will be necessary at home. Regardless of the dream, the structures must help make it happen. By revisiting the structures you will be able to ensure your dream does not die or fade away as the process evolves.

While you are in this part of the work, take time to reflect. You know your life best and you will be able to assess what you need to have in place for you. Consider who might be able to help you. However, in order to have anyone else honour the goals you have set, you must first honour them yourself. It is important that you commit to following through on the actions before you ask that of anyone else. In determining appropriate structures you may also want to analyze past successes. It is helpful to understand which routines and activities worked in your life. How did these structures shift, as you got closer to the goal? Did the support structures cause a shift in you? Sometimes structures can provide clarity; they can be the catalyst for an internal transformation that causes you to get clear about a goal as well as really want it. As this transformation occurs, the momentum starts to build and you start to see results.

In addition to the supports, you still need to be on guard for infiltration of harmful organisms and wasted energy in the garden. Gardeners have to be vigilant for weeds and even parts of the plant that may not be serving it well. Weeding and careful pruning are also important parts of being successful. Sometimes even if the right seeds are planted, other growth can take over or impact achievement of the beautiful blooms.

THE WEEDING AND PRUNING ACTIVITY

This next exercise is about identifying some of the actions and thoughts that might be poisoning or hurting your garden or goals. I call these harmful actions and thoughts *weeds*. In this activity, reflect on the aspects of your life that you have chosen and complete the following sentences.

In my goal area I have noticed that the biggest stumbling blocks that I allow to get in the way are...

In my goal area I seem to be engaging in physical or mental self-sabotage when I...

In my goal area I allow others to sabotage my goals when...

Conversations that are weeds are usually about...

Knowing what my goals are, it seems I allow weeds to grow when I...

These are just a few of the kinds of weeding statements you can create. Take your time and allow yourself several iterations as you are working towards your goals. Remember, in the garden, weeding does not all happen in one afternoon. Thoughtful analysis takes both energy and time. It is sometimes better to work on weeding in smaller patches than tackling all of it at once. Look for things that have choked out your dreams in the past. Look for the weeds that have robbed you of passion in the goal area.

Once you have identified a weed, your job is then to get rid of it. This sometimes means making a decision not to engage in a thought process or activity. In other cases, you may need to go back to the supports activity and build in an additional support for this goal. For instance, you may find that you get into a certain conversation with a specific person and it always seems to get you off track with your goal. Notice I did not give you an option of calling people weeds. People can contribute to your weeds either intentionally or unintentionally through their words or actions. If a person says something to you that is a weed for you, then that is what you need to work on shifting. Decide whether engaging in specific conversations are useful or productive for you. Alternatively, you may want to develop a strategy for refocusing what is discussed or for how a conversation goes.

Sample:

Aspect: Health (wellness and weight loss)

In my goal area I have noticed the biggest stumbling blocks that I allow to get in my way are my own procrastination, being swayed by fads and what seems to be working for others, rather than what is right for me. I can be more focused on losing weight and looking good than actually being healthy.

In my goal area I seem to be engaging in physical self-sabotage when I " reward" myself with bad food when I show any signs of weight loss or success and when I fill up my life so it is impossible for me to adhere to the schedule that was set for exercise.

In my goal area I seem to be engaging in mental self-sabotage when I look in the mirror and see myself as never getting back to the great body I once had and when I compare myself to others and feel like a failure.

In my goal area I allow others to sabotage my goals when I let them stray from my program to one of their "quick fix" weight-loss routines. I am tempted by the fast results and end up feeling frustrated when they don't work for me.

Conversations that are weeds are usually about how skinny someone looks or how fat I look, both of which seem to leave me feeling discouraged about ever achieving my goals.

Knowing my goals, I seem to be allowing weeds to grow when I collapse the weight loss and wellness into one single goal and when I judge my success against that of others.

Going back to my supports, I need to be strong enough to thank well-intentioned friends for their advice about what I should do. I can acknowledge that it might have worked for them but I have to commit to what works for me, and it is about being well not just losing weight. I have a set diet and exercise routine, and I need to commit to that rather than look for shortcuts. I need to remind myself that I have a vision of a body that I had twenty years ago, and it may be unrealistic to engage in that mental comparison. I also need to remind myself I want a healthy body not necessarily a skinny body.

Remember the weeding activity is not about beating yourself up for what you have allowed in your life. Even the most beautiful gardens will have some weeds. The purpose of this activity is to identify the weeds, determine what allows those weeds to thrive and prevent those things from happening, and determine how you can keep the weeds from taking hold in the future.

You may go through several passes of the weeding activity as you start to evaluate your life; assessing the weed as well as how it is thriving may give you some insights on how to address the weed. That is another purpose of the Establishing Supports activity. In a garden, the knee-jerk reaction to a weed is to just pull it out; however, sometimes that does not result in long-term success (you may have left a very strong root that just comes back with a vengeance later on). Gardeners need to balance the reactive state with some more proactive behaviours. Sometimes you need to guard against the weeds. In other cases you need to strengthen the plants in the garden. The Establishing Supports Activity is actually a combination of addressing the weeds and also giving strength to the plants in your garden. Establishing your supports is about addressing some of the things that have shifted in your way of being; you may need to consider removing things such as distracting activities, de-energizing habits, and negative thoughts from your life. Be on guard against these weeds should they creep back in (think blackberry bushes and bamboo!). Keep focus on what you have shored up, as weeding can sometimes cause you to lose sight of what was important in your garden. Once you have removed a weed, replace it with some positive thoughts and behaviours that move you closer to your goal rather than further away.

The pruning aspect of this activity is a little different. When pruning you are not looking for toxicity or invaders in your garden, but rather you refine the focus and actions towards your goal as you move towards it by eliminating activities that do not support you in meeting your goal. In the metaphor, a gardener may remove suckers from a tomato plant. These side shoots from a main stem are removed so that the nutrients remain focused on a few strong branches and ultimately provide larger fruit. Leaving the suckers still allows the plant to grow, but the energy is scattered and thinly spread through all the different branches. Pruning provides a higher yield. In the same way you can evaluate the activities that have crept into your process and are drawing energy away from achieving the goal you envisioned. Decide whether those *side shoots* (i.e., repercussions or resulting activities) are necessary or appropriate. For example, if you set a wellness goal and decided to join a running club, you would have established structures when you signed up, invested in good running shoes, and cleared your schedule for the training times. You might have worked on weeding out the conversations with doubters who wondered if you could even complete a race and focused on spending time with those who cheered you on. Having done all this, you start to spend extra time with the your fellow runners after each training session. Although spending extra time with the runners is encouraging for you, it has become a more social experience than one about achieving your weekly targets. This side-shoot activity has put pressure on your other commitments. You are now considering giving up the runs because you are feeling the conflicting demands on your time building up. Removing this sucker means getting clear that the time you invest is about running, and that a ten or fifteen minute unwind or debrief is sufficient and lets you honour the other obligations in your life. In a way, pruning is building a structure with commitment to actions. Being on guard for side shoots helps you stay focused on your original commitment.

These weeding and pruning activities continue throughout your journey towards your goal. You may find that you spend considerable time with this chapter or come back to it as milestones are achieved. Revisiting this chapter is a good way of ensuring you have kept your structures up to date and are frequently examining what needs pruning or weeding.

If you are wavering about doing this work, you may want to go back to the very beginning of the book where you decided whether you were *really, really* ready. Gardening can sometimes feel like hard work; depending upon the goals you chose, you may have moments where you feel overwhelmed. Use these weeding and pruning activities as a way of reevaluating what is going on, and consider going to Chapter 7 if you are feeling stuck in a rut or are feeling dispassionate about this process. Once you start achieving results and are benefitting from the routines and activities that you have committed to, you will find that you have started the process of reigniting passion. Even small wins are pivotal in creating the momentum that feeds your passion and helps you maintain your excitement for achieving your goals.

There is one more activity to consider in this chapter, especially if you find yourself second-guessing your commitment or what it will take to achieve your goals. This may look like a "cost of doing nothing" exercise; however, examining the cost of not gardening also allows you to explore another part of yourself—your core vulnerability—and may shed some light on other reasons why you have not achieved your goals in the past.

THE COST OF NOT GARDENING ACTIVITY

Go back to your goals and seed packets. Consider the aspect of your life that you have identified, focusing on those aspects in which you have set goals. Complete these sentences as you reflect on your life:

My real dream in this aspect of my life is to…. (goal)

Real success and happiness in this area means… (seed packet)

I would be really sad if I never…

My core vulnerability or fear in this area is…

Having completed the sentences, consider what you have written. Look at the words objectively, as if it was not you who wrote them. What do the sentences tell you about this person? What is important to this person and what is his or her key vulnerability? If you have done this activity in an authentic way you will start to see a deeper version of you. These are the drivers of what is important to you and also what might be the basis of your fears and anxieties.

There are two reasons for doing the Cost of Not Gardening Activity. Firstly, this activity helps you to reconcile your real passion with your goals. Hopefully, your new goals bring you closer to what would really make you happy, rather than what you think should make you happy. Secondly, this activity may help you identify some of the fears or concerns that have prevented you from succeeding in the past. Complete the Cost of Not Gardening Activity and after you have objectively reflected on what was written and established an insight about that person, record those insights in your journal or personal record. Imagine you are reading about someone else and record your reflections about this other person: What do the sentences tell you about this person? Remember to take into consideration this person's goal and key fear or vulnerability.

Sample:

Aspect: Friendship

My dream in this aspect of my life is to have a few friends that are real than a whole entourage of acquaintances.

Real success and happiness in this area would be to have friends who really know me.

It would be really sad if my friends did not know how much I appreciated them.

My core vulnerability or fear in this area is to die alone.

Objective Insights: True or authentic friendships are important to this person and the fear of being alone may side track the development of true friendships to developing a larger number of acquaintances.

Aspect: Expression of Creativity in Music

My dream in this aspect of my life is to be good enough to jam with a band.

Real success and happiness in this area would be that I did not care what others think of my playing, I just played.

It would be really sad if I never tried to play a musical instrument.

My core vulnerability or fear in this area is that I would be terrible and embarrass myself.

Objective Insights: This person has a specific dream in the area of music and may be most blocked by the evaluation of others.

Having completed the Cost of Not Gardening Activity, you can now zero in on a key plug or barrier to connecting with your passionate self. Now the trick is to face this vulnerability head on.

Years ago, I ran a leadership retreat for a local police agency. The purpose of this retreat was to help the officers and civilian staff work better as a team. Part of the session was looking at the question, "Who are we in the face of failure?" Although most of the challenges and activities were with teams and groups, parts of their course required them to do some of their own introspection.

In one activity, the group was taken to an outdoor high ropes course where they were challenged to overcome their fear of heights and explore their willingness to trust others. I was the facilitator for the session and one member of the group challenged me to participate in at least one exercise. In that moment, I was confronted with my own extreme fear of heights. As the retreat leader I assumed I would be facilitating from the ground; I had never really thought about having to engage in this activity myself! I took the risk that I would end up as a blubbering mess in the fetal position, I paired up with another participant, and up we went. At the time it seemed to be one of the scariest situations I had ever intentionally put myself in, but through the activity and upon successful completion, I had a profound insights about my fear of heights—it was all a game in my own head. My fear of heights was something I had allowed myself to be talked into. The outdoor high ropes course was quite safe, yet I was treating it as if it were very unsafe. I had years of self-talk that had convinced me that I should be terrified, which resulted in me reacting as if I was engaging in something extremely dangerous. When I really thought about it, the high ropes were not so frightening. Facing that core vulnerability allowed me to push past it and look at it in a much more reasonable light. Conquering that fear was extremely empowering. I felt like I could do anything! I realized that my unfounded fear was just self-talk that had gone wild. The energy that I had wasted in maintaining that fear was now available to me, and I felt as if it had made me a stronger person.

In a similar way, I now ask you to look at your core vulnerabilities and see if there is an idea, concept, or fear that you are holding that can be defused or overcome. For example, if you have a fear of rejection, perhaps it is helpful to remember that no matter what you do, everyone will have an opinion about it. Is it more important what you think of yourself or what others think of you? For those that have a fear of being alone, we have to remember that ultimately we are only alone when we look at our human form—that is how we came into this world and whether or not people are by our sides, that is how we will leave the world. Alone is only fearful if you have not taken the time to get to know yourself and recognize your interconnectedness with the rest of the universe. For those of us of who are fearful of being hurt or unloved, again it is important to remember that if we have self-love and a connection with an all-loving spirit that love will never be far from our lives.

One support you may consider to conquer a vulnerability is through a release in which you mentally let go of your fear. For you this may begin by bravely putting yourself into a situation where you confront your fear. Remember to be objective about the real risk; would someone else see this as unsafe or is it self-talk? Before the letting go can truly happen, you must understand your vulnerabilities at the deepest level, but doing so will be like shedding huge weights off of your being. In many religions, meditation or silence creates the opportunity to go quietly within. This activity involves doing a bit of *housecleaning* by clearing out the negative or toxic thoughts of the mind and spirit that may be impacting behaviour or creating unwarranted anxiety or worry. This clearing allows you to be in a state that is more complete. The housecleaning helps reduce the self-talk and helps keep future weeds and toxicity at bay.

All of the activities and reflections in this chapter should support you as you work towards your goals. Come back to this chapter and the activities to ensure you are addressing the evolution of your process. Remind yourself that being complete allows you to have a better understanding of your true self. You will see your true passion and what provides you with joy and contentment unfold before you, and you will start to enjoy watching your garden grow.

Chapter 5 Activities

> **DO**: Complete the Establishing Supports and Weeding and Pruning Activities. When pruning, you may want to do several passes by examining each life area separately or by working on one goal at a time. Establish some time frames for when you will come back to these exercises. Consider using specific milestones as opportunities to revisit the work of this chapter. Record the routines and timeframes in your journal.

> **REFLECT**: Observe what came out of the two activities—what structures or supports were the result of your weeding and pruning? Consider past successes and the structures that have served you well. Consider which structures have not served you well.

> **DO**: Complete the Cost of Not Gardening Activity. Try to write it as objectively as possible. Evaluate what you have

89

written from a third-party perspective. What insights do you have about this person given what you have read?

➤ **REFLECT**: What is your core vulnerability? What makes you feel the most afraid or anxious? See if you can push past this fear or anxiety to regain the energy that is wasted in perpetuating this fear. What can you take to challenge this vulnerability and conquer it?

➤ **DO**: Share at least one of your goals, seed packets, and structures with someone who knows you. If you are ready for advice, listen openly. Record any insights in your Bright Sparks section of your journal or personal record.

Chapter 6: The garden is within the gardener.

As you continue delving within, you will find that you are coming closer and closer to your true self. This kind of self-evaluation is like peeling the layers of an onion. Self-evaluation takes time, and each of the activities throughout the chapters to this point have encouraged you to go a little deeper and get to the next layer of *you*. This chapter addresses some of the final activities you may complete in discovering the core of your being. Going within means finding the *real gardener,* not just your true self, but also the source that created you. Tapping into this helps ensure you will reignite your passion in a powerful and connected way. Tapping into your true self also means that you will have a better understanding of the layers you have peeled away, of what may have prevented you from succeeding before, and of what you will need to move past in making this connection with your true self now.

Your core, your true self, has existed in you since you were created. Your core has been a constant, and although it may have been hidden, you can be assured that your core is still there. In this work you may have started to have glimpses of your true self, but it is time to forge a stronger connection. In chapter 3 you were asked to consider when you disconnected from the rest of the world. This often happens at a very young age. Not only does a disconnection happen on the outside, I believe this also happens on the inside. In the time when you learned the word "me" and "mine" you created the beginnings of a boundary for yourself in the universe. When you separate yourself from the universe and are not an integral part of it, then it becomes difficult to draw from the universal energy. Understanding your true self and the real gardener allows you to recognize the tremendous power source that is within you. When you are aligned or in synch with this source, it fuels the growth in your garden in a way that outshines all the weeding, planting, and nurturing that was undertaken by you in a physical way. The strength received from being aligned with the universal source takes the simple activities presented in this book and transforms them into something magical. You must understand that establishing goals, creating "to do" lists, and the physical activities are not all that are required to build dreams; there is more to it. There is a passion within that energizes all of your labour with a wave that is nothing short of magnificent.

In the garden, the power source is nature. The gardener may sow the seeds but if they are planted in winter they will not tap into the force that creates ideal growing conditions. When the gardener understands and accepts the power of nature and aligns to it, this communion supercharges all the gardener's labour. As you go within you will begin to understand the true connection you have with the universe. There are no boundaries. The universe is interconnected. This means you and I are both connected with everyone else. When you find the core of yourself, you will start to see that your core is identical to everyone else's. We are all created from the same source and, therefore, what is at your core is the same as what is at mine. You will be able to know you have really seen it when the goodness that you see in yourself is exactly the same as what you see in others.

The litmus test for whether you have gone deep enough is how you look at your connection with humanity and the universe. If you still see yourself as separate, you must go further. If you accept the premise that you are a bundle of millions of atoms floating within the millions of millions of atoms in the universe and that these atoms are constantly moving and being exchanged, then it means that at any given moment what was in the air around you, is now a part of you, and what might have been a part of you is now outside of you in the rest of the universe. What you may think separates you physically from the world is a mere layer of skin, but even that is made up atoms that are constantly moving, constantly being exchanged. Despite the fact that you are not physically separated from the universe, your ego still creates a psychological separation. It was your ego that kicked in when you were young and convinced you that you were separate and alone. It is your ego that convinces you that you can do things by yourself and that you are separate from others. Your ego may try to prevent you from getting through those last layers and finally connecting with your true self and the current that connects you to the universe.

So, how do you get past this barrier? Ridding yourself of the ego is a tall order; it will fight you every step of the way! Taming your ego is a better place to start. Accepting that you have an ego is accepting your human condition. Looking past your ego allows the ego to exist, but does not give it the same power. Doing this gives you a better glimpse of what is behind the ego. It is like looking through a dirty window. Once you look past the film that has built up over your lifetime, you start to see the real you. The work that you have done in the book so far is about cleaning the window or about focusing on what is beyond.

Once you start to really see beyond your ego, you experience a profound transformation. When you are clear on the connection with the rest of the universe, you will never want to harm others as you see it as no different than harming yourself, stealing from others is stealing from yourself, and loving others is loving yourself.

This also changes your reflection of the world from *outside-in* to *inside-out*. An outside-in reflection is an ego-based activity. You perceive the world and decide how it impacts you. Your focus is primarily self-serving. Conversely, with an inside-out reflection you first go within, become complete, and take your complete and whole self out into the universe. This inside-out perspective is source serving; you put your complete self out in the universe to give and receive. Self via source is more connected, more powerful, and much less about your ego.

For an example of this, look at the motivation you may have for volunteer work or community service. There is nothing wrong with you admitting that you get a lot out of it. However, you need to ask yourself, is this really an ego activity? Are you doing the work because of how it makes you look to others? Are you doing it because it will look good on a resume? Or are you doing this because you are clear about your gifts and talents and would like to share them with those around you? You may have started the work for one of the first two reasons, which are primarily outside-in reflections. However, for many people, volunteering leads them to the third reason, which is an inside-out perspective. Volunteers who experience the inside-out process not only translate their passion into much more meaningful outcomes on the outside, but they also usually walk away with much more for themselves on the inside in terms of energy and enthusiasm.

In the garden, there are a number of reasons why a gardener undertakes gardening. Is it because it will be a source of pride and prestige? Is it for the recognition or accolades? Does it feed a sense of superiority or position? Or is it because by looking within, the gardener uncovered talents that could be manifested into something that brings joy not only to the gardener, but also for all those who visit the garden? Is this work a celebration of the gifts of the source? Gardening with the motivation to feed the ego can still make the garden a success, but the work will not be connected with true self and, therefore, may not result in a truly reignited passion. There are enough successful, unhappy people in the world to provide evidence of that. Peeling the layer of ego away will help uncover a path to a deeper level of contentedness.

A way to identify whether your ego is affected is to ask the questions: Would I do this if did not get paid? Would I do this if no one knew I did it? Would I do this if no one noticed? Other ego-identifying questions might relate to how you take credit for the work: Do you label this activity as *me* or *mine*? Does the *me* or *my* conversation separate you from the world, or does it let you contribute to it? Does your contribution have to be recognized or would you do this anonymously?

Complete the Gardener in the Greenhouse Activity and determine if you can distinguish between the outside-in and inside-out conversations. By doing this, you will shift your focus towards one that will more easily align with your passion. These two exercises will help you peel away the last layer and see more clearly what lies beyond your ego. Once you have done the Gardener in the Greenhouse Activity, carry on with the Ego in the Greenhouse Activity that follows.

THE GARDENER IN THE GREENHOUSE ACTIVITY

In this activity, imagine that *you* are now in a greenhouse. Look at the goals that you have written for yourself and the action plans you have created. Now, act as if you are an observer of this person. What is this person's motivation? Why does this person want this goal? Is this person motivated by his or her ego (outside-in perspective) and mostly self-serving? Or is this person motivated by a connection with true passion (inside–out perspective) and how this act or action is a gift to others?

What is this person's real reason for engaging in this goal? What is the prime driver of the goal? Is this goal feeding this person's ego? Record what you observe objectively. Now, is there a way you can peel away a layer to shift this from the outside-in to the inside-out perspective?

In your analysis, challenge yourself to dig deeper to find a version of this goal that can authentically be from inside-out. Do not feel frustrated if you do not uncover the true goal in one pass; your ego is present and it may want you to think you are done. Keep looking past the self-talk and feelings of sadness, anger, frustration, and righteousness. See if you can uncover how you can be connected to source in each of your goal areas. You will know you are close to your core or true self when the distracting emotions shed only to yield love. When you feel like you have found an inside-out moment, record it as a statement.

Sample Analysis:

Goal: Look after my aging father

One of my prime drivers is guilt. I do not feel this is an inside-out process, as I feel that it drains me and does not make me at all passionate about what I do.

Peeling away the guilt, and perhaps the concern about what would people say if I didn't look after dad, is a recognition that my father brought me up, brought me into this world, and is now is as vulnerable as I was when I was young.

Inside-out statement: I need to give love instead of being the receiver of love.

Record this inside-out statement, as it will be something you will need to read when your ego tries to convince you of returning to an outside-in process. Your ego will try to make it about you. When you have recorded a statement about giving love or sharing your passion, create a new seed packet that includes an inside-out line for each of your goals.

Example Revised Seed Packet

> Goal: My father is
> cared for in the final
> years of his life.
>
> Inside-out Statement:
> I do this because I
> love him.

THE EGO IN THE GREENHOUSE ACTIVITY

You will find that as you come closer to the core of yourself the descriptions of your seed packets become quite simple. This is how it is meant to be as connection to source brings simplicity into your life. However, you will need to be on guard for the ego stepping back into the process and causing a flip back to an outside-in perspective. Your ego can create fear, doubt, worry and concern, and suddenly your motivation becomes primarily about you again. Remember that when you are having *me* or *my* conversations, your ego has taken charge again.

To really see the distinction between the ego and your true self, take a moment and put yourself back in the greenhouse. Observe yourself as you did in the Gardener in the Greenhouse Activity. As you did before, watch that person, as an observer. Look at the person as separate from you. Observe the work this person has done on the journey. Get clear on your observation of this person in your mind's eye.

Now, consider that the person you are looking at is not all of you. _You_, the real you, is both the observer and the observed. Can you imagine that? The observer is part of the _real you_. Watching or looking down, you can see the ego for all that it is—it is not you! The ego belongs with the human version of you, but the real you is a combination of what you see and the one doing the watching. This may be difficult to understand at first, and your ego will not want you to make this distinction. In fact, the ego will try its best to convince you that the real you is the one in the greenhouse. The gardener in the greenhouse is human and the ego takes its natural place there. Keep observing your ego self and practice this observation. The core of you, your real self, has the ability to observe in a separate way. The real you also has the most direct connection with source. The real you has access to this source. The real you is this source.

You are the observer. The Sufi poet, Jalalud'din Rumi, encourages us to escape the prison of ego and the tangle of fear-based thinking by living in silence. The observer is silent. Quietly, you can observe all that you are in your being. When you watch from above the greenhouse, you can observe ego without judgment. As there is no judgment, the ego does not need to defend its existence. The observer can guide the gardener to source, to the gardener's true self. The observer can guide the gardener to reignite any passion by tapping into the eternal spring of source.

The Ego in the Greenhouse Activity is not meant to be only a journal activity. For this one, I encourage you to observe yourself as a daily practice. As you undertake your life (including your goals), stop and observe from above. Observe in silence. Challenge the question of connection to source and then provide the guidance to your gardener. Do not force the connection just lead it to the source. The ego tamed will lay down long enough for this connection to be established if you stay outside of the greenhouse. Success may take on a different colour or flavour for you now. Accept this new perspective of success as your evolution.

Sample Reflection:

I am challenged by the move from ego to self. Ego and self meld easily in my work, and I lose sight of myself. I commit to start my workday with a 10-minute silence, my walk from the car to my office, where I become the observer and reflect on my motivation and re-establish the inside-out perspective.

Being honest with your self at this point is critical. This is very private work, and it can leave you feeling a bit vulnerable. Some people have never had a real look inside themselves, and when they do look inside, it can be a bit overwhelming. Being with what you see—observing it, accepting it, and not judging or labelling it—is important. Honestly, one of the first times I did this work myself, I was completely overwhelmed by the type of person I saw in the greenhouse. I looked at my family and wondered how they ever tolerated me! It took a while to take it all in and to reconcile that this version of myself had a lifetime of stories, insecurities, and self-talk that had hidden the real me. Looking at my ego and how it disguised itself and justified actions, I felt sorry for those around me and guilty about how my incompletion had been something I made others carry. When I accepted that my family and friends loved me anyways, I turned a corner. I was able to receive that love for myself and start to explore the inside-out process in a meaningful way. This process started with my desire to achieve a connection to my true self and my willingness to be vulnerable while undergoing this microscopic work.

Another way to keep ego in check is to consider gratitude. In the achievement of your goals whom do you thank? Is this you and your work? There is no doubt a portion of the work is yours; however, when you start to connect with the rest of the universe you start to identify all of the influences that created you in your form. When you start to consider those that you would like to thank, you may go to the positive influences in your life that have helped you on your path. However, you may also want to consider the less than positive influences too, as they may have been your best teachers. Your seemingly negative influences may have given you clarity of self, and they may have sparked the passion for you to begin this journey. So be in gratitude for everyone and everything that has brought you to this point—your parents and family, your friends and community, your enemies and your doubters. Finally, none of this would be possible without the source that created you and the entire universe. Be in gratitude for the source.

As I look around at my garden, there is so much to be grateful for. I am thankful for all that it gives me in its beauty and inspiration. I am grateful for its imperfection; accepting the imperfection makes it easier for me to forgive myself for my flaws. I am grateful for the bamboo and the blackberries that remind me what you want in life will take work and cannot be left alone for too long. I am grateful that the garden attracts beauty in all its forms and in all the visitors that come to the garden. Most of all, I am thankful for the *real* creator of the garden.

Gratitude is the gift that keeps on giving. In the metaphor the garden as well as the gardener will be in gratitude for all that have contributed to the garden's beauty. When a gardener gets it right, aligns with nature, and cares for the garden well, it will show. The garden will show its gratitude in the blooms and fruits it produces. Within these blooms lie the seeds to sprout thousands of other gardens. Your gift of gratitude may sow the seeds of inspiration further than you can ever imagine. Within each seed of genuine gratitude lies the source ready to emerge from abundance once it has been planted in fertile soil. Though the gardener may not know where the seeds will end up, the benefits are countless and exponential. Gratitude may come in the serving of source by regenerating the ability to reproduce the garden. In your journal, take some time for the Gratitude Activity.

THE GRATITUDE ACTIVITY

Review the example below and complete the phrases as they apply to each of your goal areas. Be grateful for everyone and everything that has brought you this far, and try to be as complete as you can. Consider areas where you have not felt gratitude before or easily. Push past any negative feelings (watch the ego in the greenhouse) and find gratitude in these areas as well.

Gratitude Example

Goal:

That my father is cared for in the final years of his life.

I am grateful to him for giving me a good life within the confines of his own challenges.

I am grateful for the time I have had with him, when I know so many others that have lost their dads or their parents too soon.

Though it is has been hard, I am grateful for having moved past my feelings of abandonment, so I can be the person I was meant to be and not the bitter person I was becoming.

I am grateful for this chance to give and to have my family work through how we will give together.

I am grateful I no longer make what I give conditional. This is not a service to bill or a debt to repay. I do not need to have my father or anyone thank me. I chose to do this anyways.

By recognizing that your path may also be the inspiration for others, you give back to the source by giving back the inspiration. This level of giving, when it is unconditional and complete, gives you a phenomenal level of joy and satisfaction. You will never want to look back. When this is done, the work towards to goals becomes easier. None of it really feels like work anymore. Once the rhythm of nature is understood, the gardener naturally and effortlessly aligns to it. Once you clear the path to recognizing and understanding your true self, the connection to your goals becomes a natural extension of who you are.

Chapter 6 Activities

- ➤ **DO**: Complete the Gardener in the Greenhouse Activity. Push yourself to peel away the layers of ego. Look to achieve a statement that connects you to the giving source. Rewrite your seed packet to include the inside-out statement, and try to keep the seed packet descriptions as simple as possible.

> **REFLECT**: How has your self-talk shifted? Remember that your ego knows you well and will use clever disguises. Continue to evaluate whether you have flipped back to an outside-in perspective.

> **DO**: Complete the Ego in the Greenhouse Activity. How did this activity feel for you? Consider making it a daily practice to silently observe yourself. Identify regular times in your schedule where you have a few minutes of silence to observe (e.g., walking from your car to your office, in a evening meditation).

> **REFLECT**: Has your definition of success or happiness started to evolve in any way? What has caused this?

> **DO**: Complete the Gratitude Activity and consider where you will plant these seeds. Acknowledge and appreciate those to whom you are grateful. Be careful not to make this anything more than an acknowledgement. A thank you must be given with no expectation of anything in return. Once you are comfortable in making this just about your gratitude (watch your ego), then consider having gratitude be part of your daily practice as well.

> **DO**: Record any insights in your Bright Sparks section of your journal or personal record.

Chapter 7: How do you make it through a dispassionate time?

As you progress through this book, it is important to remember that part of your work may involve overcoming challenges. Although some of the stumbling blocks have been addressed throughout the book, this chapter may be helpful as a refresher or if you need additional help with a particular challenge. I like to think of this chapter as the one that can truly help you find "peace through the process." Learning and transforming can be painful and tumultuous. If you are not clear on what I mean, recall when you learned how to ride a bike. The concrete was a very powerful teacher of balance and chances are you had a few scrapes and tears through the process. The same can be said for just about any learning that requires the building of skill, knowledge, or insights. Often, learning is not easy. This chapter will provide some general guidance about some of the stumbling blocks and common pitfalls you may experience as you proceed through this work. As both a teacher and a consultant, providing others with support and guidance during times of difficulty or challenges has been a big part of my focus. Below are some common issues that can arise and the questions and suggestions that may help you get past what is blocking you.

One of the reasons you may have come to this chapter is that you feel that the process is not working for you, or you are at a standstill. It is important to remember that you may be operating with a mindset that attaches a specific meaning to the breakdown in process. You may interpret that when things are not working then there *must* be something wrong. If that is the case, you may be limiting your awareness and, ultimately, what you are able to take out of this dispassionate time. You become focused on fixing things and making things right rather than taking the time to look at what this difficulty has to teach you. You may want to challenge yourself to review what is happening to see if there is learning in the challenge. Is there a possibility that this stumbling block is preparing you for a breakthrough?

I believe that there is always a lesson about self in discord. Feeling dispassionate can be one of your most powerful teachers. Being agitated provides the contrast for you to recognize how it feels to be at peace. I remember marveling one evening at how many more stars we were able to see while on vacation in Seychelles. We were there visiting our cousin, and we were mesmerized by a sky simply full of stars. As I compared this sky to the one we would see from our home in the city back in Canada, our cousin turned to us and said, "You need the darkness to see the stars." My first reaction was how much sense that made, but when I thought about it more I realized the beauty of the statement. I have kept this phrase close to me when I have gone through difficult times—remembering that the sweetness of success and achievement and passion is truly savored when you know what it is like not to have it.

In the garden, this is akin to *always* having a beautiful garden. It would be lovely, but it is the gardener who has seen the garden in much less glorious state who will truly appreciate its beauty. These dispassionate times may be there for you to really get a sense of appreciation of how blessed you are in your life.

Having peace in the process is not as simple as stopping what you are doing when things are unsettled and chaotic. Unfortunately, dispassionate times bring with them emotional turmoil, frustration, and a proliferation of distracting self-talk. It is important to develop the skill of recognizing this time in your learning process. These times cannot be avoided. In his book, *The Different Drum: Community Making and Peace*, Scott Peck identifies the second stage of the learning process as "chaos." Times of chaos cannot be avoided, and resisting the chaos often results in more chaos. In his book, *A New Earth*, spiritual teacher, Eckhart Tolle affirms, "What you resist, persists." Understanding and recognizing chaos as part of the learning process allows the learner to accept the situation at hand and observe it for its lessons. The learner may want to reflect on what is really being said or what is really happening. The objective observation of the process is critical to be able to move on past the stage of chaos. The challenge is that when confronted with a stumbling block, you may not be your most rational and most objective.

A good example of this is when my sister took on learning to ride a motorcycle. Despite being younger than me, she is my hero and is a pioneer in so many ways. As a policewoman, she decided she would like to join the motorcycle squad. She applied and once accepted had to go through the mandatory training. A few days into the course, I received a very simple text message from her: "I suck!" This was a perfect example of chaos; she was deep into the breakdown and had an authentic reaction to the experience of failure. Of course, this explained why the training was mandatory. Handling a 900-pound Harley was not something that should just come naturally to anyone! As she carried on, the learning started to fall into place, and she recognized that she would need to understand her own skill level to develop further. Learning was a

107

process of doing a lot wrong before she could get it right. Despite her bleak moment, she began to improve and develop the skill to a level where she believed she would actually pass. When she bought her own motorcycle to ride on her days off, I realized that she had become confident enough in her ability to actually ride for fun. Long before you demonstrate your skill with confidence, and even before you are able to demonstrate it cautiously, you may very well go through the "I suck" stage of the work. Accepting that stage with humility and maturity is one of the keys to getting past it as quickly and as smoothly as possible.

The following is a list of some common stumbling blocks. I hope that there are some suggestions or insights that will help you troubleshoot your process.

Challenge: The process is not working.

Suggestions and Insights:

- ➢ Consider that this is your frustration with the steps and how long the work might be taking. Are you allowing yourself enough time?

- ➢ Consider how you have been working through the different stages and chapters. Has it been an appropriate amount of time? Remember that a gardener will not reap the benefits without the work.

- ➢ You might feel challenged with the individual learning process. Consider reviewing how you have proceeded through the steps with a trusted friend or family member. It might be easier for you to work though this in a paired activity or even as part of a study group.

Challenge: I have stopped the work.

Suggestions and Insights:

> Have your priorities changed? You may want to go back to Chapter 1, and ask yourself if you are really and truly ready. Re-read your Gardener's Oath (see Chapter 1): Are you taking care of yourself enough to take care of the work?

> Were you confronted by something that you uncovered? Consider that you may be avoiding a conversation or an analysis that you know you need to make.

> Are the structures insufficient to support you? Review the concept of structures in Chapter 5 and determine whether your work evolved and your structures have remained the same.

> Has your ego or self-talk kicked in with doubt, fear, or frustration? Work on the Ego in the Greenhouse Activity (found in Chapter 6) and try to tame the ego enough to work past it.

> Are you writing a story about failure? Are you sabotaging your work by telling yourself, "If I stop now, I may not succeed, but I can be sure I will not fail." Review the Cost of Not Gardening Activity in Chapter 5. Can you accept a garden that does not have these goals in bloom? Will you still be passionate about your life?

Challenge: I am tired of the work.

Suggestions and Insights:

> Working in the garden can feel like a chore. This is also a normal part of the learning process. The initial excitement

of the blooms may have energized the earlier part of your work, but there is a huge space of time between planting seeds and seeing a fully developed garden. In between there is the work of tending the garden, which can sometimes feel tedious. Going back to your seed packets, remind yourself of the clear goal and of the core of your passion that drives this work. Furthermore, you may want to create some fun, joy, or even rewards for the parts that seem more mundane. For example, you may reward yourself with a dinner out for each completed chapter. Or perhaps an evening off from the work with each breakthrough.

➤ Have your priorities changed? You may want to go back to Chapter 1, and ask yourself, "Are you really and truly ready to do this work?" Re-read your Gardener's Oath (see Chapter 1): Are you taking care of yourself enough to take care of the work?

➤ Review the Cost of Not Gardening Activity from Chapter 5. Can you accept a garden that does not have these goals in bloom? Are you still passionate about your life without having achieved these goals?

➤ Are you putting too much on your plate? Are there some things that can be put on hold temporarily so that you can make more time for your goals? This is more likely to happen if you are feeling fully committed to your goal; ask yourself if this is really what you want.

Challenge: I do not have the time.

Suggestions and Insights:

- Have your priorities changed? You may want to go back to Chapter 1, and ask yourself, "Are you really and truly ready to do this work?" Re-read your Gardener's Oath (see Chapter 1): Are you taking care of yourself enough to take care of the work?

- Regardless of the reason, not having the time is a reflection of your current situation. Ask yourself if not having the time is a story you are telling yourself. A garden will not bloom if you do not make the time, so decide if you want it and how you will make the time.

- Consider that time is one of the structures that is required for your dreams to grow. How does this structure need to improve?

Challenge: What if I fail?

Suggestions and Insights:

- So what if you do fail? In Chapter 6 you were asked to be grateful for everything and everyone that brought you to where you are in your life today. Your failures have also been a part of your learning process. This book took five years to write, including two failed attempts. If I had accepted failure, I would be left with a stack of notes and the regret of not pursuing my passion. After I accepted failure as part of the journey, I was able to separate the need to write the book as my passion and the concern of failure as my ego.

> Isolate this as self-talk (recall the Greenhouse Technique introduced in Chapter 1) and carry on with describing your seed packets (see Chapter 3) anyways.

> If you have experienced failure in the process, stop and look at what you have learned. When you learn from failure, you are less likely to make the same mistake again.

> Failure may be something you are allowing others to define. Be aware that you are the only one who will decide if your garden is beautiful. Do not let others cause you to waver from your passion.

> A more powerful question that you might want to ask yourself is: "What if I succeed?"

Challenge: I am in over my head.

Suggestions and Insights:

> This process can feel quite overwhelming, and it is important not to rush it or take it on in your life when you are not ready.

> This process is not a substitute for counselling, so if you have been working with a counsellor in the past, include your counsellor in this work. If you feel that counselling may be a better option for you, trust that the work that you have done here has helped get you started on your process of personal growth and development.

> You might be challenged with the individual learning process. Consider reviewing how you have proceeded through the steps with a trusted friend or family member. It

might be easier for you to work though this in a paired activity or even as a study group.

Challenge: The activities do not work for me.

Suggestions and Insights:

➤ These are suggested activities. If you can determine a version of these activities that seems to be a better fit, then allow yourself the creativity to adapt them. Most gardeners develop their own techniques over time, as long as they are following the basic formula. Sometimes a trial-and-error process is needed to find which activity will work in a specific environment.

➤ Watch your ego—this might be a bit of self-talk coming up to sabotage your process. Ask yourself, "Why am I resisting the structure?" Is there a way you can get this done and work past what has blocked you?

➤ You have to be willing to accept the outcome of your resistance. If you do none of the work, then you cannot expect the benefits of the garden.

Challenge: I did the work and the garden did not bloom.

Suggestions and Insights:

➤ Have you rushed the process? Have you allowed for enough time? A good friend once reminded me that a bloom only flowers in the fullness of time.

➤ A gardener has a number of things to investigate when a garden has not flourished. Assess your process to see if something went astray. Did you do a Soil Assessment (see Chapter 3)? Where did you sow the seeds of your goals? Did you have adequate structures and weeding of self-talk? If you are having trouble being objective in this analysis, consider reviewing how you have proceeded through the steps with a trusted friend or family member. It might be easier for you to work though this in a paired activity or as part of a study group.

➢ A gardener must accept that every seed will not grow. It may take a while to identify what are the right seeds for your garden and how your work is best able to nurture the growing process.

➢ Consider whether you made some assumptions about the work and it being complete. Did you skim through any of the chapters?

Challenge: I do not need this work.

Suggestions and Insights:

➢ If the book outlines a process that you have already completed, perhaps you can use it to analyze how you fared. In order to "build muscle" in the application of the stages, it is important to understand the significance of the individual exercises. Use your real-life experience as your working example to assess you own progress.

➢ Consider this might be your ego or self-talk trying to prevent you from doing this work.

➢ If you have achieved a level of contentment in a certain area of your life, consider picking another aspect or area to repeat the process.

➤ This book is a guide. A gardener does not use a guide everyday; however, this guide can be a good reference when reviewing the process or approaching a different kind of garden or set of growing conditions.

Challenge: I cannot keep a separate journal.
Suggestions and Insights:

➤ Consider that this might be your ego or self-talk resisting the structure and perhaps sabotaging your work.

➤ Objectively evaluate what part of the journal is challenging you. If you could adapt this part of the process and still do the work with integrity, what would you change? Remember the journal is only one of the supports.

➤ The journal or recording area that you started with may not be the one that works throughout—consider changing it to another format.

Challenge: It is too much work.
Suggestions and Insights:

➤ Have you pushed the process? Have you allowed for enough time? Sometimes people feel overwhelmed when other parts of the life have not been appropriately prioritized. Consider whom you have asked or enrolled to support you in the process. Do you have enough support?

➤ Have your priorities changed? You may want to go back to Chapter 1, and ask yourself, "Are you really and truly ready to do this work?" Re-read your Gardener's Oath (see Chapter 1): are you taking care of yourself enough to take care of the work?

➢ Were you confronted by something that you uncovered? Consider that you are overwhelmed by a conversation or an analysis that you know you need to make.

➢ It may be that you have not yet tapped into your passion. Once you have tapped into your passion, it will likely stop feeling like work at all.

Challenge: I cannot get past the self-talk or ego.

Suggestions and Insights:

➢ This is a common problem as the self-talk or ego has been part of your identity for so long. Consider having a trusted friend or family member join you in some of the self-talk activities. Give them permission to challenge you and be compassionate but honest in their constructive coaching about what the ego or self-talk may be for you.

➢ If you are blocked by the same self-talk or the same issue over and over again. Consider that your approach has become predictable and your psyche and ego can see this coming. Work on the Ego in the Greenhouse Activity (see Chapter 6) as well as any of the Greenhouse Technique (see Chapter 1) that helped you isolate self-talk.

➢ If you feel like you are caught up in the same story over and over again, consider that this level of drama has poisoned the soil. One way to try to address this is to spend some time writing out your story. Once it is told in its entirety, in one sitting read it out loud. Read it over and over until you get sick of telling it. When you are sick of telling it, you may get sick of carrying it. Consider that this is the story you have been planting year after year. There is no room for anything else to grow. Let the story go so you can make room for something else to flourish in your garden.

Challenge: The people around me do not understand this work.

Suggestions and Insights:

> It can sometimes feel quite challenging to enroll others in your personal development process, especially if they have not walked every step of the journey with you. Be careful about the assumptions you make about others and your own judgment of their resistance.

> Although I have suggested an alternate strategy for the work to be paired or in study groups, this should be undertaken carefully. The Gardener's Oath (see Chapter 1) should include some parameters about this process. Create a structure for your goals to be successful, and do not be surprised that when it comes to the real work because you will still have to do most of it on your own. It is your garden and although you might get help along the way, it is important that you shoulder the responsibility of the blooms.

> Honour the need for others to step in and out of your process. You need to ask for help, not insist on it.

> Take the time to share your insights. Be careful not to turn your learning into a righteous conversation. Start by discussing what you have learned about yourself in the journey.

> If you have shared your goals and then subsequently experience failure, be careful of how you respond to others'

reactions. Making your work public creates vulnerability and your ego may kick in when you are confronted with stumbling blocks along the way.

Challenge: I tried many self-help books but never really get what I want.

Suggestions and Insights:

> There is an important distinction to make when committing to undergo this work. In the metaphor, you learned how to garden, but it does not guarantee the blooms. Reading the book only means that you have understood the process. This is like reading a cookbook and wondering why you are still hungry! It will be the actual doing of the activities as they relate to your specific goals that will make a difference. Otherwise, you will just repeat the same part of the process in a different format. Push yourself to identify your garden in full bloom and become passionate about your end product, not just the way to get there.

> You may be drawn to this work because it is your self, expressing a desire and readiness for this growth. Learn to listen to that and ensure you are equating it back to your passion.

Challenge: I was working on the wrong goal.

Suggestions and Insights:

> There are a number of opportunities for you to reconsider your goal (see the Seed Packet Activity found in Chapter 3). Give yourself permission to change your seed packet descriptions if your instincts tell you that you were off track.

➢ Sometimes the goals are too big or not in the right area. Remember a gardener sometimes needs to sow some seeds to determine that this is not the right plant for this environment. You may want to adapt your goal based on your evaluation of what has transpired.

Challenge: My challenges are external to me.

Suggestions and Insights:

➢ There may be times when the scales have tipped because of something that has happened outside of you. In those circumstances it is important to gauge what is still an internal tipping of your scales.

➢ Theologian Reinhold Neibuhr's prayer (also know as the "Serenity Prayer") comes to mind:

"God, grant me the serenity
To accept the things I cannot change;
Courage to change the things I can;
And wisdom to know the difference."

Sometimes this work will involve your accepting the uncontrollable circumstances that occur in your life. Look at the later chapters for more clarity on what you might be able to change.

Challenge: What if this does not make a difference?

Suggestions and Insights:

➢ Whether you make a difference may be a perceptual issue (remember the black and white card from Chapter 1). You will need to make a decision whether you are attached to the outcome or committed to the work. A gardener will garden in the hopes of having a great outcome, but accepts that the future is not entirely predictable.

➤ Consider whether this is ego or self-talk and whether you have made your passion or the discovery of your passion conditional.

I am hopeful that these suggestions and insights gave you a few ideas about what is happening and how you might get back on track with your development. For me, I can be my own biggest enemy when confronted with a stumbling block, and the self-talk can be so distracting that I completely lose track of my focus and my goal. Self-talk allows for the kind of negativity that can sabotage personal growth. Learning to monitor for this may minimize some of the unnecessary roadblocks. Accepting failure as a natural part of the process and learning to be with it can pave the way for you to proceed on with your next steps.

Chapter 7 Activities

➤ **REFLECT**: What is your relationship with stumbling blocks or failure? What do stumbling blocks and failure mean to you?

➤ **DO**: Review your progress so far and flag when you experienced the most challenges.

➤ **REFLECT**: Are there any patterns to where things breakdown? What are the types of breakdown that are common for you?

➤ **DO**: Record the key lessons you learned about yourself when you experienced a challenge in the process. In the bicycle metaphor, when learning how to ride, what was your concrete?

➤ **REFLECT**: Consider what you can do to have better peace through the process. Will changing your mindset make a difference?

➤ **DO**: Record any insights in your Bright Sparks section of your journal or personal record.

Chapter 8: Creating the openness to choose a passionate life.

At this point you may have recognized that finding your passion is not about thinking it up. Your passion has always existed. Hopefully, through the work in the previous chapters, you have found that rediscovering your passion is more about clearing out what has been in the way rather than it is about hunting for or creating that passion. This work is about releasing stories you spent your lifetime telling yourself or hearing from others. Discovering your passion is accomplished by uncovering the core that is you and that has always been you, and it is about understanding who you are, what is important to you, and how you reconcile all of that in your life.

I have often seen a dramatic shift in people when their perception changes. As they rethink and reevaluate some aspects of their lives they experience quantum shifts in their existence. Outside of them, those changes may not be quite so visible. They essentially look like exactly the same people. They are doing the same job, living with the same family, and are engaging in the same activities each day. However, *who they are being* has shifted so deeply that when you look a little closer it seems you are seeing them for the first time. For others the work has meant big changes—both inside and out—in the type of work they do, their life priorities, or in their personal relationships.

The level of change or transformation that you have experienced may not be an indicator of whether the process has worked, but rather a sign of the growth you were ready for at this time. To have a better understanding of how your life has been impacted you may want to couple your assessment in what has shifted with the happiness indicators you established in the Garden Assessment Activity in Chapter 2.

When you start to evaluate your progress, remember also to take the time to be in gratitude. This work, like your life, is not a race; winning is not determined by when you get to the end. Slow down and savour your life and the passion you have uncovered. In the summer that I wrote the manuscript for this book, I was able to do so in a way that made the summer amazing. I had weeded out a lot of the usual frenetic activities that would fill a summer and spent most of my time writing or being with my family. Sure there were many other things I could have been doing, but when I got clear that my family and this manuscript were the two things I would like to focus on over those weeks, suddenly everything else started to fade away. I had a deep sense of gratitude for the work that I loved and a family that I was blessed to call my own. I savoured each day; for the first time in longer than I can remember, the summer actually slowed down. My summer did not whiz by in a flash, but instead was days on end of just being in contentment. When you take the time to be grateful, your awareness of what is around you and even how time passes you may change for you.

As you reflect on your progress, you may wonder about what is next. Where will you go from here? That is really up to you. As you move forward, it may be that you want to continue the work in the areas you chose and explore them further. Conversely, you may want to move to other aspects of your life. For example, having sorted out some of the priorities in your work, you may decide it is time to look at the relationships in some of the other areas of your life. Take the time to consider your next steps carefully. Now that you have the formula and you have seen how it works, it will be up to you to decide where you will work next in your garden.

Coming back to the same work after some time may also provide you with different insights. This could be because you may be on another part of your own journey. Students who take the same course with me years later often have the experience of *hearing* the content differently. I believe this is because their own growth has caused an evolution in the goals they set for themselves. Their lives or priorities may have changed. These life changes impact how these returning students listen, which points them to different areas of work and development. In the garden, you made some priorities or goals. When the techniques were applied, hopefully the results were achieved in the harvest or blooms. Revisiting the work is remembering that your garden is yours for many seasons. In subsequent years you may come back to an area to improve on it further or because it seems like the right focus for you. Remember that revisiting the work may result in new and different outcomes; the garden itself continues to evolve. Accepting that the garden itself is constantly changing allows you to remain open to learning, even in areas where you have had significant development.

Life today is complicated; if sorting through your life was a simple process then a book or course to help you reignite your passion would be unnecessary. The path that you take is not necessarily predictable. Hopefully, completing this work helped to alleviate the fear and anxiety of whether you are on track. Just doing portions of this work starts to shift this fear. Knowing that you are living an intentional life and that you have given careful thought to your priorities and goals can create a level of calm that can quiet your restless or searching mind.

Accepting discord is also part of the process. As the previous chapter revealed, accepting chaos may be a critical part of your development, so make sure you do not to avoid it. Chaos may show up in many stages of the process, early in the work as a sign that something needs to change or later on as a precursor to a breakthrough or an insight. There is usually a reason for discord, and if you accept that fact, chances are you will find it less distracting. In the garden, the seedling or bud must put a tremendous amount of pressure on the seed coat or flower casing before it can break through. With growth comes transformation. It is inevitable. If you can look at the discord in your life with the mindset that it is a natural part of your evolution, you will not be so focused on making it go away. You can be with it and look for what the discord is signaling to you. Being with the discord rather than resisting it may help you through a dispassionate time. Accepting the moment as it is helps you to find peace throughout the process.

What is exciting about this process is that you start to live in a way that you have never lived before! This process hopefully gives you the sense of being alive, awake, and passionate. The connection with this tremendous energy allows you to tap into the power that created you and helps you align yourself in harmony with everything around you.

This work will be ongoing for you, and I encourage you to revisit it often as a gift to yourself and to those around you. I do this work on an ongoing basis and ask my students to revisit it as well. Share what you have learned and remember the power of giving. Look for the ways you can give of yourself to others. When you give of yourself with clarity and authenticity, I promise the benefits will come back to you. Consider the law of tenfold return. Many faiths have a basic tenet that what you give will come back to you in a much grander way. This is seen as a sign that the universe is a power of abundance. The concept of tithe was not just a tax or an obligation, but rather it is recognition of our interconnectedness. When you give of yourself, freely and unconditionally, the abundance of the universe eventually makes its way back to you. You ultimately end up giving to yourself—not as a strategy but as a natural consequence. Some people call this karma. You set in motion the universe realigning itself to you. When you have tapped into your passion and give joyously from that place your passion will enrich all that is around you and come back and reward and refuel that passion. If you hold on and come from place of scarcity, the law of tenfold will still hold and scarcity will be all around you. This is what I think Albert Einstein meant in his famous quote, "The most important question we will ask of ourselves is do we live in a friendly or hostile universe?" Whatever your answer, it will be true. Your answer is your reality. What you believe and what you put out into the universe is ultimately what you receive. It is all up to you. It has always been all up to you.

Chapter 8 Activities

> **REFLECT**: Review your goals from the beginning of the book, where have you gotten in them? How did they shift?

How have you made a difference in the world around you? How can you be in gratitude for this? As you get connected to your passion, what can you give to those around you?

➤ **DO**: Share your overall journey with someone you trust. Record any insights in your Bright Sparks section of your journal or personal record.

➤ **REFLECT**: Who were your teachers in the journey? What did they teach you? Consider how you might acknowledge them.

➤ **DO**: Engage in an expression of gratitude. Now consider making an expression of gratitude a daily practice.

➤ **DO**: Engage in giving of your self freely and unconditionally. Now consider making unconditional giving a daily practice.

➤ **DO**: Sit back and enjoy your garden!

Final Words

I thank you for courageously taking on your life and have deep gratitude for your trusting me along the way. I am in awe of what is created when people align with their passion and am humbled that you have allowed me to be a part of your journey and a part of building your phenomenal garden. May you live an amazing life and be blessed in every step of your journey.

Made in the USA
Charleston, SC
14 November 2014